ROBERT E. ALEXANDER
3657 SO. LA BREA AVENUE • LOS ANGELES 16, CALIFORNIA

D0594510

TWO-THIRDS OF A NATION
A HOUSING PROGRAM

TWO-THIRDS
OF A
NATION

A HOUSING PROGRAM

BY
NATHAN STRAUS

1952

Alfred A Knopf   NEW YORK

HD
7293
S87
1952

L. C. catalog card number: 51–11991

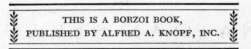

THIS IS A BORZOI BOOK,
PUBLISHED BY ALFRED A. KNOPF, INC.

Copyright 1951 by Nathan Straus. All rights reserved. No part of this book may be reproduced in any form without permission in writing from the publisher, except by a reviewer who may quote brief passages and reproduce not more than three illustrations in a review to be printed in a magazine or newspaper. Published simultaneously in Canada by McClelland & Stewart Limited. Manufactured in the United States of America.

FIRST EDITION

To the Memory of the Pioneers

JACOB RIIS (1849–1914)
AUTHOR OF
How the Other Half Lives

SIR RAYMOND UNWIN (1863–1940)
AUTHOR OF
Nothing Gained by Overcrowding!

EDITH ELMER WOOD (1871–1945)
AUTHOR OF
Slums and Blighted Areas in the U. S.
(Published by the Federal Emergency Administration of Public
Works as Housing Bulletin #1, 1935)

ROBERT F. WAGNER (1877–   )
*Sponsor of the United States Housing Act of 1937,
which established the first permanent low-rent housing
program in United States history*

*For to famous men all the earth is a sepulchre: and
their virtues shall be testified, not only by the in-
scription in stone at home, but by an unwritten record of the mind, which more than any monument
will remain with every one forever.*
THUCYDIDES (471–400 B.C.) *Pericles' Funeral Oration*

Criticism in a free man's country is made on certain assumptions, one of which is the assumption that the government belongs to the people and is at all times subject to the people's correction and criticism—correction and criticism such as a man gives, and should give, those who represent him and undertake to act on his behalf. Criticism of the government made upon that basis is proper criticism, no matter how abusive.

But abuse of a representative government made, not upon that assumption, but upon the assumption that the government is one thing and the people another—that the President is one thing and the people who elected the President another —that the Congress is one thing and the people who elected the Congress another—that the executive departments are one thing and the people whom the departments serve another—abuse of a representative government made with the implication that the government is something outside the people, or opposed to the people, something the people should fear and hate—abuse of that kind is not criticism and no amount of editorial self-justification can make it sound as though it were.

ARCHIBALD MACLEISH

Foreword

AMERICA today stands committed to a rehousing program with the goal of providing a good home for every family in the nation.

The threat of war, or war itself, may delay the rehousing of slum families; shortages of manpower may disrupt new construction schedules; plans for defending our cities may take priority over plans for rebuilding them. But there can be no turning back. As age relentlessly takes its toll of existing homes and the population continues to grow, the ranks of the homeless and ill-housed will multiply year by year. Postponement can only sharpen the problem.

World conditions may enforce delays in construction. They should not delay study and planning. America has much to learn in the field of urban redevelopment. The extra time may be turned to good use.

Under these circumstances, there is need for a book which sets forth the fundamentals of sound housing policy. The book should deal with existing conditions and should be factual and prophetic, rather than historic.

Above all, the book should be written with an eye constant to the ultimate goal. This goal is not "slum clearance," "homes for veterans," or "a building boom." Those are all kindred subjects. They bear about the same relationship to the real problem as a bull fight to the sausage business. They deal with the same raw materials—but in different ways.

The real goal is nothing less than a comfortable home for every American family. This means the poor as well as the rich, the descendants of those who crossed the Atlantic in the slave galleys as well as the heirs of those who made it on the Mayflower.

Acknowledgments

ONE of the pleasant aspects of writing a book is to discover how many people are ready to give of their time and thought to help the author. It is a source of satisfaction to write this acknowledgment of my indebtedness to some who are friends and to some who are complete strangers. Each of them contributed to the interest and the accuracy, as well as what I hope will prove the usefulness of this volume.

For criticism, editorial suggestions, and other advice, I want to express my special thanks to Fred Berger, Alexander L. Crosby, William F. Dufty, Leo Goodman, secretary of the National Housing Committee of the CIO, Louis Kronenberger, Asher B. Lans, and Herman Ranes.

John P. Dean's book, *Home Ownership: Is It Sound?*, has proved an invaluable source in writing the chapter on that subject.

For much of the material embodied in the chapter on prefabrication I am deeply indebted to Burnham Kelly, director of the Albert Farwell Bemis Foundation of the Massachusetts Institute of Technology and the author of *The Prefabrication of Houses*. John J. O'Brien, president of Gunnison Homes, Inc., and James R. Price, president of National Homes Corporation, generously supplied additional information. I hasten to add that none of these gentlemen has read the chapter as it appears here and doubtless they would disagree with many of the opinions expressed.

To Frank C. Montero, director of the Urban League Fund, I am indebted for permission to reproduce an excellent graph.

I want to thank Austin J. Tobin, executive director of the Port of New York Authority, for allowing me to use his statistical material in writing of tax exempt government bonds, and the National Child Labor Committee for supplying historical material on that subject.

The distinguished authority on city planning, Lewis Mumford, not only has allowed me to quote liberally from his articles in *The New Yorker*, but has given me the benefit of his criticism in writing the chapter on *Urban Redevelopment*.

Leon H. Keyserling, formerly Deputy Administrator and General Counsel of the United States Housing Authority and now Chairman of the President's Council of Economic Advisers, has reviewed some of the chapters and made invaluable suggestions as to form and content. The opinions expressed, however, are by no means uniformly in agreement with his own.

My daughters-in-law, Rebecca S. Straus and Ellen S. Straus, have helped by their frank criticisms to make this a more readable book.

These acknowledgments would be incomplete without mention of the assistance rendered by young men and women who must be nameless. I refer to the students in my class at the City College of New York in 1949 and those whom I taught at Columbia University in 1950 and 1951. Class discussions of most of the chapters in the book contributed new points of view, refreshing criticism, and some excellent advice.

Last, but by no means least, the work done in research

and in revising and typing by my able editorial assistant, Lucy Booker, and in checking of figures and statistics by my loyal secretary, Elizabeth M. Rogan, deserves far more than this inadequate expression of thanks.

It must be emphasized, at the risk of repetition, that none of those named should be held responsible for any views or opinions expressed herein—although such merit as the book has is due largely to their generous assistance.

Contents

TWO-THIRDS OF A NATION
A HOUSING PROGRAM

I. *Need versus Deed*

1

THIS is a book about housing, and housing is an old problem of mankind.

Was the great turning point in history the discovery of fire? The invention of the wheel? Probably not. Both were milestones on the road.

The turn occurred when the first man broke ground with his crude plow to plant the first seed. Up to that moment, man had been a nomad, a wanderer. When he began to till the soil, he anchored himself to one spot. He had to stay to tend the crops and reap what he had sown. The hunter or the herdsman had been satisfied to live in a cave or a tent. The farmer wanted a house. And the housing problem was born.

From the dawn of history until today the housing problem has been with us. Though unsolved, it is not insoluble. We have the techniques, the experience, and the financial resources needed to provide every American family with a good home. We can do it—and we must do it.

"Housing affords the best single opportunity for that very important blending of private enterprise, local initia-

tive, and forward-looking public endeavor at all levels of
government which is the unique hallmark of the dynamic
American economy and which can prove to more and
more people throughout the world that our system is the
best system." [1]

2

One of our most cherished beliefs is that American production meets the needs of everybody. This does not mean
that every family can have everything it wants, or even
thinks it needs, but, rather, that a family of average income can afford the necessities of life and more of the
luxuries than an average family elsewhere in the world.
Our pride in this achievement of American free enterprise
has much justification.

Through the ages, the three basic human needs have
remained unchanged: food, clothing, shelter.

Americans probably enjoy more abundant and varied
foods than any other people in history. The very poor may
be restricted to a monotonous and inadequate diet, millions of average income may be doomed, through ignorance of food preparation, to unpalatable daily fare; but
Americans generally are well fed. Moreover, we are making steady progress in providing more and better food for
all, including those of the lowest income.

[1] Leon H. Keyserling, Chairman of the President's Council of Economic Advisers, in a speech on November 16, 1949.

If we are relatively well fed, we are even better clothed. Most Americans can afford to buy attractive, durable clothing. Some, of course, are still in rags. Some children must still go barefoot to school. Yet a human being in tatters is an unusual sight. Americans may rightfully claim to be the best-dressed nation on earth.

But when we come to the third of life's basic needs, the contrast is startling. Millions of families live in indescribable squalor. Slums and blighted areas are common to every American community. The sight of slums has become so familiar that the eye is dulled and the mind has long accepted slum housing as unavoidable even if unattractive.

Yet slum housing is a totally unnecessary evil.

Why, then, has it endured? People do not live by choice in dilapidated, overcrowded firetraps.

If better housing were available for the same low rentals, slum families would move out and owners of empty buildings would be forced to tear them down and seek other uses for the sites. Slums exist because they are the best we have to offer millions of families. Every American slum mocks the idea that private enterprise meets the real need for human shelter.

The failure of private enterprise goes far beyond its inability to wipe out our slums. Actually few new homes are built within reach of middle-income families. Young married couples do not double up by choice with in-laws and friends. A big airy room in a respectable boarding house is still not the dream of the middle-income bride.

When discharged veterans returned by the thousands after the War, an increase in doubling up was unavoidable. Many people believe that this condition has improved. *The fact is that almost a million more families were living doubled up when the Housing Act of 1949 was passed than in 1945.*[1] At the beginning of the Korean crisis, there were more than two million families living doubled up—about the same number as there were immediately after World War II. There was, in reality, no justification for the belief that housing conditions had improved in the five years between. What was mistaken for progress was but a treadmill. There remained as much overcrowding and doubling up as ever.

During the post-war years when adequate housing construction might have reduced the shortage, American building enterprise failed. The homeless, the doubled up, felt a justified sense of frustration as it became clear that —except for the wealthiest income group—the housing shortage was to be a permanent feature of American life.

World War II, often cited as the cause of it all, was not chiefly responsible. It merely served to aggravate and intensify a long-existing deficiency. *At no time in the twentieth century has our annual production of homes kept pace with the growing population and the real need for shelter.*

People concerned with appalling conditions in the

---

[1] Statements by certain elements in the real estate fraternity have hardly been in accord with the facts. For instance, Boyd T. Barnard of Philadelphia, former president of the National Association of Real Estate Boards, at the very time the shortage was most acute, said: "There is overconsumption of our existing space. We have several million people who, because of frozen rents, are able to buy more housing space than their income would normally allow. Approximately a million and a half living units which were designed for two or more people are now occupied by only one person because of frozen rents. Everybody knows cases of this kind. The stenographer who used to live with another girl now has her own individual apartment." (*New York Herald Tribune,* October 13, 1946.)

slums often forget about the hardships of middle-income families. Overcrowding is just as bad for the family of the salesman, the bookkeeper, the taxicab driver, the civil service employee, the schoolteacher, or the young doctor as it is for the family of the unskilled laborer.

Two-thirds of all the families in the country have incomes of less than $80 a week. Their need for new homes is a pressing and often insoluble problem for them. It should be the concern of all of us.

3

In recent years the housing industry has developed an alarming new trend. The homes it produces are growing smaller and smaller. A one-family house or apartment used to be overcrowded when two families moved into it. Today's typical homes are overcrowded with *one* family— if there happen to be two children of opposite sex.

"Efficiency units and single-bedroom apartments account for well over two-thirds of the FHA [Federal Housing Administration] approvals. . . . Fewer than a third of the planned apartments thus are suitable for families with children. . . . In Houston, only 2 per cent of the units had two bedrooms. In Chicago, less than 10 per cent had two bedrooms. . . .

"At less than $60 a month, only the Southern cities offered many new apartments. Washington, New York, Indianapolis, San Francisco, Denver, and Seattle had no units planned at rentals under $60. For that price, families could find virtually no new apartments in Philadelphia, Chicago, and Los Angeles. . . . All this indicates that the apartment boom has been doing little or nothing for families with average incomes." [1]

Charles Abrams sums up the problem: "While private housing is being built on a boom basis for the top-income group, and a token slum-clearance and rehousing program has been begun for the lowest income group, most families will benefit from neither program.

"What is needed is a complete program for the lowest and middle income groups; the share-cropper, the migrant worker, the elderly, the slum dwellers displaced by slum clearance and urban redevelopment, cooperative buyers, underprivileged families who want to own homes, veterans stranded in trailers and temporary houses. These are the great forgotten families of America.

"Virtually all of our new private houses are 'economy houses,' built for a mythical average family with no more than two children of the same sex who are supposed to share a common bedroom.

"We are building no houses for the large family, the one-person family, the aged couples or individuals. Yet little Denmark has had a program for housing the elderly since 1891 and more than 500 comfortable apartment houses provide decent housing in this little country. Sweden, Norway, and England have similar programs. We alone, of the democracies, lag behind."

---

[1] *U. S. News & World Report*, May 5, 1950, pp. 36, 37.

4

An adequate housing program should envisage the whole life of the individual, inside the house as well as outside. The home should provide a setting for his development as an emotionally balanced and mature human being. Good housing should include quiet parks for adults as well as playgrounds, the noisier the better, for youth. There should be community rooms for dances and parties and for meetings where neighbors may practice the art of debate which lies at the very root of democratic government. Not least important, there should be space for hobbies.

Mechanized and urbanized life tends to deny man the satisfaction of creating something. Over the last quarter of a century, Americans have become a nation of spectators. We are lookers rather than doers. It requires no statistics to prove that *watching* baseball, football, hockey, and prize fights has increasingly become the chief recreation of millions. Going to the movies, watching a television screen, or looking at comic books may be forms of harmless recreation. But vicarious activity can never be a real substitute for sports and hobbies as a means of developing character and promoting contentment.

No housing program can be considered complete unless it provides opportunities for active and satisfying use of leisure. Repairing a piece of old furniture or playing in an amateur band, digging in a garden or tying flies for fishing, may be better balm for the soul than even the fanciest new household gadget.

5

Tradition requires every book on housing to begin by defining a slum. Next come statistics on crime, juvenile delinquency, disease, infant mortality, and loss of life in slum fires. All of this is intended to prove that slums are objectionable.

It would seem that the time has come to dispense with these usual preliminaries. If the American people did not know the meaning of the word "slum" or were not aware of the effect of slums on human well-being, the Housing Act of 1949 would never have become law. If the devastating effect of blighted areas on people—and on real estate values—had not been proved and re-proved a hundred times, no comprehensive housing program would have been enacted by the Congress. It is hard to believe that anyone would say of the families in the slums today, as a respected Congressman did in 1938: "They are living in shacks and hovels because God made them unable to earn more." [1] It seems no more necessary to argue the case against the slum than to argue the case against cancer.

---

[1] Representative Robert Luce (Republican) of Massachusetts before the House of Representatives Committee on Banking and Currency hearing on Amendments to the U. S. Housing Act of 1937 on May 4, 1938, p. 92.

The Housing Act of 1949 says: "The general welfare and security of the nation and the health and living standards of the people require . . . the realization as soon as feasible of the goal of a decent home and a suitable living environment for every American family."

Most people know that the large cities do not provide homes that meet these standards for all the inhabitants. In New York City for instance, there are more than 50,000 occupied "old-law" tenements. They are buildings of a type which it has been illegal to erect since 1900. So they are all more than half a century old. These slums are called "home" by about 1,470,000 people or about one-sixth of the city's population. Of course, they are foci of crime, juvenile delinquency, and disease. Built of dried out wood, the buildings would offer ideal fodder for demolition and incendiary bombs.

A committee of citizens making a tour of one section of the slums in the fall of 1950 found that "At 1247 Park Avenue, between Ninety-sixth and Ninety-seventh Streets, eight Puerto Rican families were living in tiny rooms in the cellar . . . the rent was $30 a month. There was one filthy toilet for the eight families and everything was gloomy. This is one block from Park Avenue wealth . . .

"At 121 East 109th Street, a man and his wife and their nine children were living in three small rooms for which they said they paid $60 a month. At 1786 Lexington Avenue the group climbed some dingy stairs and entered an apartment where eight families were each living in a small room. Some paid $11 a week and some paid $7. There was one kitchen for the eight families.

"At 530 West Forty-fifth Street, two families were living in a two-room apartment. There was neither gas nor electricity because the occupants couldn't pay for it. They used kerosene lamps and cooked on a kerosene stove." [1]

It is pleasant to accept the fiction that such conditions are to be found only in New York and a few other large cities. The fact is that more than 20% of the inhabitants of practically every town and city of the U. S. A. live in similar conditions. In rural areas, the percentage of unfit housing is higher than in the towns.

Nine million American families will go home tonight to sleep in substandard dwellings. "Substandard" means (a) lacking private toilets or (b) lacking running water or (c) having only cold running water or (d) so dilapidated as to endanger the health and safety of the occupants.

How decent is the housing in *your* town, how suitable the environment? One way to find out is to take a walk and employ what Albert Einstein calls "the holy curiosity of inquiry." Pick a neighborhood you have never visited on foot, the kind known as "poor." Make sure that you inspect the halls and stairways and that you see *inside* some of the apartments—where people *live*. This is essential for real enlightenment. All of the buildings that look like slums deserve that description, inside and out. However, many exteriors that seem not unattractive are deceiving. Within, the housing may be bad.

Before you start on your journey of exploration, try to get rid of the blind spot that tends to make us all believe that existing conditions are "normal" or "unavoidable." This is especially true when our own home town is the subject of investigation. The first step toward enlightenment is a determination to see housing conditions as a stranger would.

---

[1] *New York Herald Tribune,* October 19, 1950.

A few hours spent, with open eyes and an open mind, in inspecting the low-rent areas of any city, town, or village in the United States will convince anybody that a large percentage of his neighbors lack "a decent home" and "a suitable living environment."

If you found such conditions in a *foreign* country you would surely question whether the government was fostering loyalty and good citizenship by condemning its people to live in misery and squalor. You would ask yourself whether youth of both sexes, crowded into housing which provides no privacy indoors and no play space out, were apt to develop into law-abiding citizens.

This is what the victims themselves think about the system, as told to a judge in a Brooklyn courtroom: "A teen-age gang member with a pimpled face and long, stringy black hair got on his feet in Kings County Court today and told a shocked judge and jury exactly why underprivileged kids join gangs and hate cops. Just turned 20, Joseph Senatore chewed gum violently and talked out of the side of his mouth, the way he learned to do while serving three years for burglary. But he shot his words out hard and fast, like sharp punches.

" 'Look, your honor, it's not us kids. It's the neighborhood. It's the environment. We ain't got no place to go. Do you want us to stay home seven nights a week? Look, we go into a pool room or something, and the cops break in on us and separate us. We got no place to go.' " [1]

Boys whose only playground is the street where it is "against the law" to play ball soon learn to fear and hate the policeman on the beat.

---

[1] *New York World-Telegram & Sun*, November 22, 1950.

6

_____

If you care to dig a little deeper into conditions in your home community, you probably will make some inquiries about rents. When you do, you will be astonished at how little most families pay for shelter. You knew, of course, that rents were low in the worst slums—often $10 a month or less. But probably you did not know that middle-income families seldom pay more than $50 a month. If you check up on one hundred families, you will find that eighty of them pay less than $50. At least those are the figures for the nation as a whole.[1]

Now, with that figure of $50 fresh in your mind, you may decide to visit some of the new housing under construction. A four-room apartment? Why, certainly—$80 to $115 a month. Next, try a development of little box-like houses, the kind that are mushrooming in nearly every city.[2] You will find that the real monthly cost to a buyer is about the same.[3]

_____

[1] The average rent for all dwellings in the United States was $39. The average for urban dwellings was $41. (From Report Series 8C5, No. 1, February 1951, Bureau of the Census.)

[2] "Slums of the future are already being built in many urban fringe areas where inadequate housing has been thrown up to meet overwhelming demands. Major public health problems are being created in these areas. Built outside the limits of the central city, housing in these fringe areas lacks adequate zoning, building, and sanitary controls." (Dr. Leonard A. Scheele, Surgeon General, U. S. Public Health Service, in a talk before members of the National Association of Housing Officials in Boston, November 14, 1949.)

[3] See Chapter IV.

You now have plenty of food for thought. The cheapest new housing in your community costs $80 or more a month. But for two out of three families the limit is about $60. Even with the aid of FHA-insured loans, the housing built today, whether for rent or for sale, is beyond the means of two-thirds of the population. The conditions in your own community are not unique; they are duplicated in every part of the United States.[1]

North, south, east, and west, in the cities, in the suburbs and on the farms, there is practically no new housing produced by private enterprise at a figure the average American family can afford. That fact is the hard core of the housing problem. Any discussion that ignores or dodges that fact is worthless.

---

[1] This has been confirmed by many independent investigations.

A committee of the New York State legislature reported: "Barely any of the housing provided by unaided private operation at current rentals would be available to the veterans of the city."

According to the Philadelphia Housing Association survey made in December, 1948: "Two-thirds of all families are priced out of the market because their incomes are less than $4000 a year, and 99³⁄₁₀ per cent of homes sell above their purchasing capacity."

The report of the Housing Authority of Savannah (Georgia) for 1949 states: "In the 20-month period from January 1946 to September 1947, private builders erected 701 houses for white families. Records of the city building inspector show that the average cost in 1946 was $4125; in 1947, $7375. The 78 per cent increase is explained chiefly by the builders' preference for marketing higher-priced houses. This preference is understandable and legitimate, for there's more profit in the most expensive houses. But it means that families of low and moderate income cannot expect to get new private housing."

According to "H. E. Riley, chief of the division of construction statistics of the Bureau of Labor Statistics, in a survey of new housebuilding in the New York–New Jersey metropolitan area: only 5% of the houses coming up are expected to sell for under $7500." (*Wall Street Journal*, July 16, 1951.) This is equivalent to a statement that 95% of the new houses built in the New York–New Jersey metropolitan area in 1951 are beyond the means of half the population.

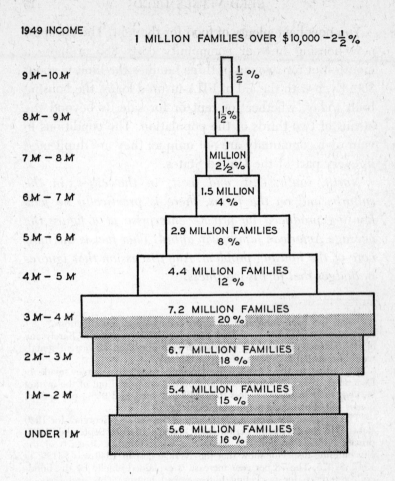

1949 INCOME

1 MILLION FAMILIES OVER $10,000 — $2\frac{1}{2}$%

1949 INCOME	
9 M – 10 M	$\frac{1}{2}$%
8 M – 9 M	$1\frac{1}{2}$%
7 M – 8 M	1 MILLION $2\frac{1}{2}$%
6 M – 7 M	1.5 MILLION 4%
5 M – 6 M	2.9 MILLION FAMILIES 8%
4 M – 5 M	4.4 MILLION FAMILIES 12%
3 M – 4 M	7.2 MILLION FAMILIES 20%
2 M – 3 M	6.7 MILLION FAMILIES 18%
1 M – 2 M	5.4 MILLION FAMILIES 15%
UNDER 1 M	5.6 MILLION FAMILIES 16%

Practically no new housing that meets minimum standards of sanitation and space—whether for rent or for sale—is within the means of families in the shaded portion of the graph.

SOURCE: *U. S. Dept. of Commerce,*
Bureau of the Census. (*1950 Census*)

7

Suppose you confront a builder or a real estate man with this fact. He will probably reply about like this:

"Plenty of housing is being built for high-income families, probably more than is needed. This means that, when the new construction is completed, families that can afford $85 or $100 a month or more will move in. The housing they now occupy will then become vacant. If the old houses are large, they may be altered to accommodate more tenants of lower income. But, in any case, they will be available for families that cannot afford new housing. Over the years the homes built for the wealthy filter down to the middle-income group and eventually even to low-income families."

This line of argument, the so-called "filtering down theory," has long been used as a second line of defense by spokesmen for the real estate interests. The argument sounds plausible. Let us suppose that you decide to test it by personal investigation.

You visit an area of second-hand "mansions" in your home town. Many of the old residences of the wealthy have been converted into rooming houses. The big home where the bank president lived in 1890 has now become a rooming house for four families. Other dwellings built to meet the needs of one family with many servants have been altered to accommodate five or even ten families. Gas plates and cheap partitions have been installed to justify the label of "kitchen apartments." The alterations, made at minimum expense to provide maximum income for the owner, rarely offer anything that could be described as good housing. In justice to the owners of the buildings, it must be pointed out that no amount of ingenuity could have accomplished that miracle.

The filtering down theory would not be tolerated in any other field of merchandising. If you went to an automobile dealer with $1800 to buy a new car, and he told you he could offer nothing but a five-year-old Cadillac, you would be indignant. If the automobile industry produced nothing but cars costing $4000 or more, how long would the average family have to wait before such cars "filtered down" to its buying level? And by that time how satisfactory would be the transportation provided by these aged vehicles?

Consider clothing. Suppose the minimum price for a new suit were $80 and that men able to pay only $35 had to wait until a suit filtered down from the backs of the rich. The clothing manufacturers would scarcely claim that, by producing a surplus of $80 suits, they were helping the people in rags. As a matter of fact, the filtering down theory is less valid for houses than for clothes. An expensive suit made for a rich man, size 40, can be altered to fit a poor man, size 40. But a superannuated dwelling designed for one wealthy family and its servants rarely can be converted into livable housing for several families of low income. The unhappy product of the attempt usually degenerates into a slum.

The filtering down theory has never worked in the past. It will never work in the future. Hand-me-down housing is no answer to the housing problem.

8

Because housing and family income are so clearly related, it is usual to discuss housing problems in terms of a rather arbitrary division of the population into three income groups.

The top-income third, the 12 million families in the United States with incomes of more than $4000 a year, have enough new housing provided by private building enterprise. In this field, architects and builders have made a record of fine achievement. Even allowing for much uninspired architecture and shoddy construction, the American home at its best offers charm, comfort, and ingenious adaptation to the conditions of modern life.

The middle-income third comprises families with incomes of from $2500 to $4000 a year. For the great bulk of these families, and obviously for all of those in the lowest-income third, with incomes of less than $2500 a year, practically no new housing is built, either for rent or for sale. The need for shelter of families *outside* of the wealthiest income third offers the greatest opportunity for an expanded program of home building—an opportunity that private enterprise has proved helpless to exploit.

Because private builders provide homes for only a small wealthy segment of the population, residential construction quickly finds its market glutted. This threat so alarms

the National Association of Real Estate Boards and the
U. S. Savings and Loan League that their publicity organizations proceed to grind out prophecies of impending
doom.

Morton Bodfish, chairman of the executive committee
of the U. S. Savings and Loan League, in opposing an increase in housing construction said: "If we keep up a
million-a-year pace for as much as five years, we're going
to have houses running out of our ears." [1] Henry A. Bubb,
Topeka, Kansas, president of the League, stated: "Nine
hundred thousand to one million units a year are being
built, but we'll soon have to slow down even this pace." [2]

If such views were to prevail, slums would continue to
grow and all of the American people, excepting a small
wealthy group at the top would experience increasing difficulty in finding places to live.

In most years the building industry does produce
enough new homes to meet the needs of the wealthy or
the well-to-do. In some years it provides more than
enough. This period of swollen profits for speculative
builders ends abruptly when the supply of new high-
priced homes exceeds the number that wealthy families
can absorb. The volume of residential building begins to
dwindle. Jobs in construction trades disappear entailing
large-scale unemployment. Lay-offs in an important segment of the economy are felt in curtailed demand for
goods of all kinds. Depression creeps upon the nation. The
home building industry is a boom-and-bust industry because two-thirds of its potential customers are priced out
of the market.

---

[1] *The New York Sun,* November 19, 1949.
[2] *New York World-Telegram,* November 19, 1949.

Fluctuations in economic conditions do not substantially change this picture. Rents and incomes tend to rise and fall together. In the lush late 1920s as in the somber early 1930s, the gap between the cost of shelter and the rent-paying ability of home seekers was about the same. Incomes are higher as this is written than they were in the pre-rearmament post-war years—but the cost of new housing is higher, too.

Whether two-thirds of American families have annual incomes of "less than $4000" or "less than $4100" or "less than $3900," it is safe to predict that private building enterprise, as constituted and financed today, will fail to produce new homes within their means. *Incomes change, housing costs change, but the gap between incomes and housing costs remains unchanged.*

9

What is the real need for new housing over the next ten years? National income is about double the highest in pre-war history. The population has increased by 19 million, or 15%, since 1940. Indications are that the rate of population increase in the 1940s will be maintained in the 1950s. We would then need at least 5 million new homes merely to take care of the population increase with no allowance for obsolescence or replacement of slums.

To enable families now living doubled up to find separate dwellings, to replace slums, and to keep up with population increase, the United States needs 17,600,000 dwellings. The breakdown is:[1]

HOUSING NEED, 1951–1960

Net increase in families, plus 3% vacancy allowance	4,000,000 [2]
Families now seeking separate dwellings	2,100,000 [3]
To replace nonfarm slums and blighted areas:	
Dwellings warranting demolition now	7,000,000 [4]
Dwellings that will become seriously substandard in the next 13 years	2,000,000 [5]
To replace the most seriously substandard farm homes	2,000,000 [6]
To replace dwellings destroyed by fire, storm, flood, or public works other than planned redevelopment	500,000 [7]
TOTAL DWELLINGS NEEDED, 1951 THROUGH 1960	17,600,000
(or: 1,760,000 additional units per year)	

---

[1] Table compiled by Catherine Bauer in a pamphlet, *A Housing Program for Now and Later*, National Housing Conference, Washington, D. C., p. 16.

[2] United States Census Series P-46, No. 4.

[3] The United States Census estimated, on the basis of 1947 surveys, that about 2,750,000 married couples were living in other families' households and that another 500,000 families were occupying transient or nonfamily quarters. It is here conservatively estimated that only about two-thirds of these 3,250,000 families are actually seeking separate dwellings, but it may well be over-optimistic to assume that more than a million families are living "voluntarily" under such conditions.

[4] Includes seriously substandard nonfarm dwellings, variously estimated at 6 to 10 million, minus an allowance for scattered dwellings that might be repaired, plus an allowance for relatively standard dwellings that would have to be included in any large-scale clearance and redevelopment operation. See *America's Needs and Resources* by J. Frederic Dewhurst and Associates (Twentieth Century Fund; 1947), chapter on "Housing" and census material.

[5] Estimated on the basis of .5% of existing supply per year.

[6] A minimum 10-year program to meet the need, estimated by the Department of Agriculture.

[7] *America's Needs and Resources*, Chapter 8, page 166, op. cit.

The key to success in meeting—quantitatively and qualitatively—real housing needs is to be sought in bridging the gap between what Americans can afford to pay for shelter and the cost of new housing. Thus, the first step toward solving the problem is to understand the nature of housing costs and the factors that determine them.

II. *The Cost of Housing*

1

HALF the human race goes to bed hungry every night. In whole sections of the world, human beings clad in rags arouse no special comment. Housing, like everything else, is miserable. Family incomes are too low to provide food, clothing, *or* shelter for many of the people.

But in America, millions of well-fed, well-dressed families live in slums.[1] Bad housing persists because good housing costs too much. Architects, builders, planners, and public officials may differ on almost every other aspect of the housing problem, but on this they agree: housing costs are too high. Most discussions of housing begin with an attempt to assign blame for this condition—and end with a search for the villain.

To the builder, the villain is the labor union. To the labor leader, the villain is the ever-present threat of un-

---

[1] New York City has 9000 acres of "genuine recognized slums." (Report of the Mayor's Committee on Slum Clearance by Private Capital, January 23, 1950.)

Washington, D. C., has 44,000 dwellings "which do not meet civilized standards of safety, health, and fitness for human habitation." (Report of the National Capitol Housing Authority.)

employment. To many economists, the villain is the bad organization of the construction industry. Others pick on the high cost of city land, still others point to antiquated building codes. There is a measure of truth, of course, in all these accusations.

The builder points out that skilled mechanics earn more per day than the man who is to live in the house. He cites union contracts and regulations that prevent him from using the most efficient construction techniques. He complains that workers try to make every building job last as long as possible. So—the villain must be the labor union.

The labor leader knows that the volume of building construction fluctuates violently from year to year. Because of the feast-and-famine nature of the industry, building trades workers face weeks of idleness in most years. Hence the insistence on a high hourly wage. The mason who lays too many bricks may be speeding the day that he will lose his job. Hence, "featherbedding" and the slow-down—labor's weapons to thwart the villain of unemployment.

The economist points out that a few large concerns dominate the manufacture of brick, lumber, cement, insulating materials, plumbing fixtures, electrical equipment, and nearly everything else that goes into a house. On the other hand, the industry that utilizes these materials consists of a host of small contractors, most of whom have little capital and cling, whether by habit or by labor union pressure, to wasteful, old-fashioned building techniques. So—the villain must be something nebulous called "obsolete technology."

All these evils undoubtedly add to the cost of housing. However, if our purpose is not just to find a scapegoat but to make a real attack on costs, it would seem more constructive to define what we mean by the "cost of housing" and then proceed to analyze the factors which determine that cost.

2

The literature of housing is striking in that nearly all discussion of housing costs is focused on *construction cost*. But we pay for shelter by the week, month, or year. This recurring expense is the *real* cost of housing, and it involves many things besides the cost of construction of the building.

A tenant pays the cost of housing in a lump sum monthly. He calls it the "rent." A so-called "home owner," buying a house on the installment plan, pays many bills— some every month, others irregularly—that add up to the equivalent of a rent bill. He pays every month for interest and amortization of the mortgage; for water, garbage collection, electricity, and gas. Once or twice a year he pays for his winter supply of fuel. He pays taxes. He pays additional bills for minor repairs and maintenance expenses. The real cost of his housing is the sum of all these bills.

One of the fondest notions of home buyers is that, as owners, they will escape part of the monthly costs paid by those who rent. This, of course, is a delusion. The costs may be lumped together as "rent" or may be paid separately by a "home owner" but the same items still constitute the real cost of housing.

3

___

Whether it is a house in Maine or an apartment in California, "owned" or rented, in the city, on the farm, or suburbia in-between, the *real cost* of housing is the sum of three factors:

1. COST OF CAPITAL (Interest and amortization)
2. COST OF OPERATION (Maintenance and repairs; utilities)
3. REAL ESTATE TAXES

The relation of the total of these three items to the family income, rather than the construction cost of the house, determines the kind of housing a family can afford. Nothing less than the sum of these three items is the *whole cost* of housing.

COST OF CAPITAL

___

The *cost of capital* is the largest component in the monthly cost of housing. It accounts for not less than 40% and often as much as 55% of the monthly cost.[1] If this

___

[1] The small item of *fire insurance* is included in *cost of capital*. On a theoretical basis, this is justified because the purpose of fire insurance is to protect the value which is the basis of the loan. On a practical basis, the inclusion of insurance in *cost of capital* follows the usual custom in real estate advertisements of grouping interest, amortization and insurance together.

item could be cut in half, the cost of housing would be reduced about 25%.

Obviously the most direct way to reduce this item is to reduce the amount of money required to produce the house—cost of construction plus roads, grading, site improvement. This direct approach, however, often leads into a trap. *If building costs are reduced at the price of shoddy construction, inferior plumbing, or sacrificing space standards,*[1] *the actual monthly cost may be increased. Lack of comprehension of this basic truth lies at the root of much confusion about the housing problem.*

Reduction in the rate of interest is a direct, simple, and highly effective method of reducing the cost of housing. As Sir Ernest Simon has well stated, "The rents of houses depend more on the rate of interest than on all the other variable factors, such as cost of labour and cost of materials, taken together. . . . A progressive reduction is the most important single service the Government can render towards ensuring the success of the housing programme."[2]

Even without government insurance, the risk involved in a mortgage to produce that most essential of commodities—human shelter—should be almost negligible. With FHA insurance, the lender takes no risk whatever. He is assured of the full return of his money, with interest, over the term of the loan.

---

[1] "Economy in price is achieved by sacrificing space standards. The houses have a floor area of only 674 sq. ft. compared to the 1088 sq. ft. of a standard 6-room row house. All rooms are small. The bathroom, as a matter of fact, is so small that the door must swing out, where it obstructs the hallway. The baby's bathing equipment cannot even temporarily be accommodated in a bathroom of this size." From a description of an "economy" one-story type house built in the Philadelphia area, taken from *Issues,* published by the Philadelphia Housing Association, September–October, 1949, number.

[2] E. D. Simon: *Rebuilding Britain—A Twenty Year Plan* (London: Victor Gollancz Ltd.; 1945), pp. 226, 113.

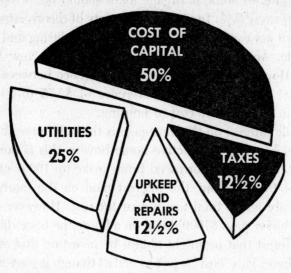

COST OF
CAPITAL
50%

UTILITIES
25%

UPKEEP
AND
REPAIRS
12½%

TAXES
12½%

This graphic picture of housing costs is intended to illustrate a principle rather than portray the cost of a typical house. No house is typical. The cost of utilities, for instance, may vary from 20% to as much as 35% of the total—and other items may vary almost as much. However, the basic truth is unchanging: the cost of housing is always made up of these same components.

The white portions of the pie show component costs hardly ever mentioned in advertisements of houses for sale, and rarely considered by home buyers.

Since all risk is removed, there is no reason why the interest rate on home mortgage loans should be as high as 4½% or even 4¼%. In view of the safety of the investment, a return not exceeding 3% would be more fitting and reasonable. According to Herman T. Stichman, New York State Housing Commissioner, the difference between 4% and 3% interest makes a difference of $2.75 to $3 per room in the monthly cost of housing.[1]

While interest on the mortgage is the only interest cost figured by most prospective home buyers, this is not the whole story. If the borrowed funds make up 100% of the cost of the dwelling, the interest paid on the mortgage obviously is the total amount of interest. However, if a home buyer pays $1000 down on a house, he is sacrificing the interest that he might obtain by investing that $1000 elsewhere. This "cost" is just as real as though it were actually paid out. The home buyer could certainly invest his money to yield about 3% so this "lost interest" should be added to the item "interest on the mortgage" in calculating monthly cost.

4

AMORTIZATION

To determine the monthly cost of a home, we must know how long it is expected to last. The length of its useful life will determine the amount of annual amortization

---

[1] *New York Herald Tribune*, September 15, 1950.

—and amortization is a key factor in the cost of housing.

The dictionary [1] defines "amortize" as: "To liquidate or extinguish an indebtedness, usually by periodic payments made to a sinking fund or to an account."

Every object we buy eventually wears out. The amortization fund consists of the money that is set aside—or should be—each year to replace the object when it is worn out.

A refrigerator has a useful life of about 15 years. If the owner kept books on a strictly business basis, he would set aside each year a sum amounting to one-fifteenth of the cost, so that when the appliance was worn out he would have on hand the price of a new one. A poorly constructed refrigerator of cheap materials might, instead of lasting 15 years, be worn out in 5 years. Obviously then, the annual cost of amortization would be one-fifth of the price paid. These simple arithmetical facts are unaffected by the bookkeeping habits of the owner of the equipment. Though he does not keep track of amortization and charge it off, this monthly "cost" is just as real and just as inescapable as though he kept accurate books.

If a $10,000 dwelling—whether it be house or apartment—has a prospective life of only 10 years, its cost must be amortized over 10 years, amounting to $1000 a year or about $83 a month. If another dwelling *costing the same amount* has a prospective life of 80 years, amortization will only amount to $125 a year—about $11 a month. Of course, the figures taken as the estimated lives of these two houses are extremes. Few dwellings are built with a life estimate either as short as 10 years or as long as 80 years.

---

[1] *The American College Dictionary:* Random House; New York, 1947–1949.

The principle, however, is the same whatever the life of the dwelling.

The monthly cost of housing is closely geared to the number of years of its useful life.

A $10,000 house with a 40-year loan at 4% interest will show lower annual cost of capital (interest and amortization) than an $8,000 house with a 25-year loan at the same interest rate because annual amortization is lower for the larger and better built home.

As long as the emphasis is on construction cost alone, the tendency of those who seek to reduce the cost of housing will be to produce an ever smaller and shoddier product. By shifting the emphasis to *annual cost*, of which interest and amortization are so large a part, the effort will be to produce a sturdier home with longer life and, therefore, lower annual charge for amortization.

The production of homes is traditionally compared with the production of automobiles. The efficiency of mass production auto building is contrasted with the antiquated handcraft techniques of home building. This comparison is unsound and it is difficult to overestimate the confusion caused by its constant use.

Aside from there being no site problem in the progress of the automobile from the assembly line to the showroom, there is an even more basic error in the analogy. An automobile is built to last only a relatively few years; a home lasts—or should last—fifty, sixty years or more. An old automobile is a worn-out, inadequate means of transportation. But an old house may be a fine, livable home.

The small town shacks and big city tenements attest the fact that much old housing is bad housing. But the point is that such dwellings were bad housing the day they were built. Shiny paint may have masked the shoddy construction or brightened the dark rooms, but most of today's slums afforded little better living conditions at five years of age than at fifty.

Age is *not* the determining factor in the merit of housing. Many of the charming and livable homes of Georgetown, D. C.; Bucks County, Pennsylvania, and Cape Cod, Mass., were built a hundred years ago. Some of the sturdy stone houses in Amsterdam, Zurich, and other European cities were built nearly two hundred years ago. These homes afforded good housing when they were built; they afford good housing today. *A well-built home, in attractive surroundings with adequate grounds, well maintained over the years, should afford desirable, livable housing for two or three generations at least.*

Actually, a house is more like a highway than like an automobile. A cheap gravel road may cost less—but, since it must be rebuilt in, say, 5 years, its amortization cost is 20% of the original cost. A first-class concrete road may cost a lot more—but, since it lasts at least 20 years, its amortization cost is only 5% annually. The little box-like house on a narrow lot is like the gravel road. Cheap to build, expensive to maintain, its limited life requires a high amortization. At no time will it provide good housing.

The well-built home of ample size, like the concrete highway, may cost much more. But it will have a long life span that justifies low amortization. Throughout its life, it will provide good living environment for people and will constitute a community asset.

5

Properly designed and constructed communities of dwellings justify a long life-expectancy. The amount of annual amortization of the mortgage should take this into account. The family that occupies the house for the first 50% of its life should not be charged 100% of the amortization.

In estimating the life-expectancy of housing, we have gone from one extreme to another. Fifty years ago it was common to assume that all housing was immortal, and depreciation zero. On such assumptions, apparently, banks holding mortgages on New York's "old law" tenements renewed the mortgages decade after decade disregarding any provision for amortization.

"The possibility of their ultimate elimination was so little considered by their owners that depreciation was seldom charged as an operating expense, and even where the net return exceeded 15%, as it often did, no provision for amortization of building cost was ever made. Mortgages on them were renewed without reduction in principal, and for many years after their construction had been forbidden, they continued to be considered prime investments." [1]

---

[1] *Report to His Honor Fiorello H. LaGuardia, Mayor of the City of New York, by the New York City Housing Authority, pursuant to Article Five of the State Housing Law, on its investigation and public hearings on living and housing conditions in the City of New York,* January 25, 1937, p. 6. The author was a member of the New York City Housing Authority which made the investigation and report.

This policy, of course, quite apart from its moral aspects, was financially unsound. Retribution, long delayed, was meted out in the depression years. There were wholesale foreclosures and some of the most respected financial institutions became the outright owners of the worst slums of New York and other cities.

The financial community, licking its wounds after this beating, went to the other extreme and became unduly suspicious of *all* housing mortgages. The FHA, set up in the depths of the depression of the 1930s, was influenced by this philosophy. It is time to re-evaluate current policies. Obsolescence should not be disregarded. Reasonable amortization of housing mortgages should be required. The emphasis, however, should be on the word "reasonable." [1]

If we are to justify low amortization, construction must be of sturdy materials with good workmanship. Rooms should be of adequate size and there should be plenty of storage space for window screens, baby carriages, bicycles, tools, heavy bedding, winter clothing, etc.

If a house is to be a desirable home 40 or 50 years from now, it should be assured of being then, as now, in a desirable neighborhood. This will require that the house be conceived as one of a group in an ample park-like setting.

---

[1] On a purely financial basis, the amount of interest paid on a loan should be reduced each year, as the loan is amortized. If this procedure were followed, however, the item of *interest and amortization* would be highest the first year after completion of the house. This has obvious disadvantages. Accordingly, the "level" plan has been generally adopted. This provides that, as the amount of interest due is reduced by repayment of the loan, the amount of amortization is increased. The annual repayment of principal is increased by the amount of decrease in interest. Thus, the home buyer, as well as the institution that makes the loan, can count upon equal payments every year until the entire mortgage has been paid up.

Landscaping should be a matter of thought and study, avoiding the pattern of identical rectangles beloved of the real estate speculator, which is at once wasteful of road space and a source of traffic accidents. There should be ample space for recreational facilities for children and adults, youth and age. The whole development should be large enough to assure permanence of neighborhood character.

Such a planned residential community will grow in beauty over the years as the landscaping, especially the trees, attain maturity. The Buhl Foundation housing project, "Chatham Village," in Pittsburgh, the first unit of which was completed in 1932, and "Hillside Homes" in the Bronx, New York City, built in 1934, are examples of graceful age.[1] There are many examples of such "old" housing, more beautiful today than the day they were completed, in Sweden, Denmark, Switzerland, and Holland.

6

To make the mistake of confusing construction cost with real cost is to take the wrong turn at a critical crossroad. Having thus started on this course, no progress is made toward the goal. For instance: if construction cost and real cost were synonymous, the wages paid to building labor would be a key factor in the cost of housing. Wages paid to labor on the site of construction amount to

---

[1] Clarence S. Stein was the architect of both of these projects.

about one-third of the total cost of a dwelling.[1] If building wages were cut in half, the cost of construction would thus be reduced about one-sixth. This, in itself, sounds like a substantial saving. However, translated into monthly cost, such a reduction in wages would effect a reduction of only about 10%.

In summary:

Cost of capital is the largest component of the monthly cost of housing and it is not determined solely by the cost of the dwelling but also by the interest rate and the period of amortization. These factors must be considered together in analyzing the effect of proposed economies in construction on the real cost of housing.

7

MAINTENANCE AND REPAIRS

Some so-called economies in construction actually *increase* the monthly *cost of operation*—the second component cost of housing.

A poor foundation means that the house will settle and the plaster will crack, resulting in a substantial repair bill. A cheap range soon wears out and must be replaced. An

---

[1] This ratio has varied little from decade to decade. According to figures of the United States Bureau of Labor Statistics, labor cost on the site constituted about one-third of construction cost in 1931–32 and also in 1946–47. (*Monthly Labor Review*, May, 1949, of the Bureau of Labor Statistics.)

inadequately water-proofed basement means quicker de-
terioriation from dampness, if not flooding in storms.
Cheap doors soon warp; cheap faucets soon drip.

A hundred dollars pared from the cost of the building
often means an added $20 a year in maintenance costs.
This extra expense may not show up during the first
years, but a house is built—and bought—in the belief
that it will last from forty to sixty years. As the decades
mount, the effect of poor construction and poor equipment will be reflected increasingly in higher bills for upkeep and repairs—increased *cost of operation.*

Maintenance and repairs—accounting for 10% to 20%
of the monthly cost of housing—are higher in cheap, jerry-
built housing and lower in soundly constructed housing of
sturdy materials. To say this seems like solemnly announc-
ing that two and two make four. Yet the general disregard
of this obvious fact prompts its restatement here. Every
wise investor in real estate knows, but few home seekers
appear to realize, that, as a general rule, the cheaper the
house the higher the repair bills.

8

UTILITIES

Cost of operation is the cost of maintaining the property
and keeping it in repair *plus* the cost of utilities.

What are utilities? They are the conveniences which
modern man requires in his home—fuel for cooking; elec-

tricity or gas for light; coal, oil, or gas to keep him warm, as well as the cost of water supply and of garbage disposal. Except in the extreme south, where little or no heating is required, utilities account for at least 25% of the monthly cost of housing. Reducing the cost of utilities is thus of great importance in any intelligent approach to reduction of housing costs.

Does cheapening the house reduce the monthly cost of utilities? Obviously not. On the contrary, a house of flimsy construction without adequate insulation will cost more to heat and the owner of such a house will soon find that he must buy a good deal more fuel, if he wants to keep the family comfortable, than his neighbor whose house is properly insulated. Insulation is invisible, but the cost of omitting it is very visible in the family budget.

As electricity is used increasingly for lighting, refrigeration, and even cooking and heating, the cost of current grows in importance. A large housing development, public or private, that can negotiate with the local utility company for electric current is in a position to achieve startling reductions in this item. The owner of a project housing 500 or more families, whether a local housing authority or a private corporation, can buy at a wholesale rate with a master meter.

An owner who is prepared to generate his own current is obviously in an excellent bargaining position. The faintest whisper of this intention has often saved many thousands of dollars.[1]

---

[1] According to the Edison Electrical Institute (Statistical Bulletin No. 16, 1948), residential rates for electric current in the whole United States averaged 3.01 cents per kilowatt-hour (1948), while according to a report (Electricity Sales Statistics) of the Tennessee Valley Authority, its rate for the same year was 1.56 cents per kilowatt-hour.

The United States Housing Authority showed how this could be done. Public housing projects, built by local housing authorities from 1937 to 1941 under the USHA program, made a striking record in cutting utility costs. Savings ranged from $2 to $8 a month.[1]

No study of housing costs is complete unless it covers the price of electricity for this is a large factor in cost and it can be reduced without any of the ill effects that attend cheese-paring in construction. Yet, in all the millions of words of publicity about housing costs issued by the National Association of Real Estate Boards, the National Association of Home Builders, and the U. S. Savings and Loan League, there is no evidence of any concern with the cost of the kilowatt.

9

TAXES

The third component of the cost of housing is the real estate tax assessed against the property. Local real estate taxes comprise from 10% to 20% of the cost of housing.

Here, at last, seems to be an item that will be decreased if the construction cost is reduced. This is indeed true under the present tax laws. But our system of levying real estate taxes is open to grave question both on grounds of economic soundness and social desirability.

---

[1] For details see: Nathan Straus: *The Seven Myths of Housing* (New York: Alfred A. Knopf; 1945), p. 121.

Real estate tax laws are a weird jumble of assessments in which it is difficult to find any underlying philosophy or theory. For instance: "The tax problem varies from community to community and is entwined with the machinations of the intricate system of suburban governments, so complex that many town officials are continually consulting maps to find out precisely where boundaries begin and end. A good example of this heterogeneous governmental set-up, as it affects taxes, is Nassau County. The county is divided into sixty-two school districts, each having its own school board whose members are elected by the voters of the district.

"The property tax for each district is determined by deducting estimated receipts—primarily state aid—from the total budget expenditures. The tax rate then is computed by dividing this tax levy by the assessed valuation of property within the district. The result is 62 different tax rates, which for the school year 1949–50, range from 57 cents to $2.25 for each $100 of assessed valuation." [1]

Local real estate taxes are collected to pay for the cost of services rendered by the government to those who live in the community. Tax funds are used for such purposes as education, street cleaning, public parks, fire and police protection, courts, jails, health centers, and hospitals. *It is relevant to inquire whether the value of these services to the occupants of a given dwelling is properly measured by the value of the dwelling.*

Slum housing is rightly considered by tax authorities to have little value. Taxes assessed against slum property are correspondingly small. Yet the cost of the very serv-

---

[1] Excerpt from a series of articles on growth of suburbs of New York City in *The New York Times* by Richard H. Parke (August 7, 1950).

ices for which taxes are collected is higher in slum areas.

Surgeon General Leonard A. Scheele states the case clearly:

"In Hartford, Connecticut, one-fourth of the population lived in poor housing and the ill-housed one-fourth produced more than half of the tuberculosis cases each year and sent nearly 40% of the city's mentally ill to state institutions.

"In the Nation's capitol, the tuberculosis death rate among the people in its squalid slums was 99% higher than for the rest of the population. The pneumonia rate was more than 25% higher.

"In Birmingham, Alabama, the rate of communicable diseases per 1,000 population was 65% higher in the blighted areas than elsewhere in the city.

"Cleveland discovered that one small slum area, occupied by less than 3% of the population, needed 8% of the city's total public health budget for the control of disease and other services.

"In Denver, the infant death rate in low-quality housing districts was more than five times that in the best districts, and juvenile deliquency was more than twice as high.

"And on the West Coast, Los Angeles' slums bred tuberculosis rates nearly 8 times higher than the better districts, and venereal disease rates 13 times higher. . . .

"A large proportion of State and local health budgets are expended in slum areas." [1]

Other costs piled by the slums on city tax budgets, although invisible and more difficult to isolate, are quite as real. There is the extra expense for fire and police

---

[1] Surgeon General Scheele, speaking at the annual meeting of the National Association of Housing Officials, Boston, November 14, 1949.

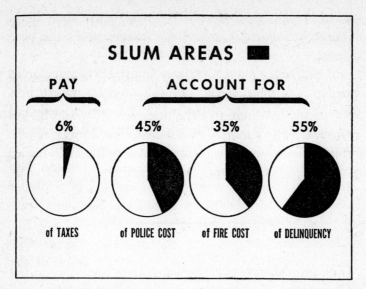

(COURTESY URBAN LEAGUE FUND)

"*Slum housing, which comprises about 20% of this country's residential areas and contains at least a third of its population, yields only 6% of the real-estate tax revenue that is the mainstay of municipal governments. In return for that 6%, slums require, on a national average, more than half of the available medical and institutional care, half the time of the police, more than a third of the time of the fire departments, and most of the welfare benefits.*" EDGAR L. JONES *and* BURKE DAVIS: "*Slum Clearance at a Profit*" *in* The Atlantic Monthly, *May, 1949.*

protection, street cleaning, and the additional expense of maintaining parks and recreational facilities elsewhere in the city for the tenants of congested overcrowded buildings. Good municipal housekeeping would dictate that the taxes assessed against slum areas should therefore be higher than the city average. This would make provision for the cost of the extra municipal services they require.[1]

The slums are the most highly subsidized housing in the United States today. This subsidy to the slum landlords is contributed by the rest of the taxpayers. It would be just as logical if the public library were to fine borrowers who returned books on time and in good condition and award prizes to vandals who tore out the pictures.

10

The present system of assessing taxes according to the value of the dwelling has even more far-reaching evil consequences. It favors the developer who constructs jerry-built housing, the kind which is destined to become the slums of tomorrow.

A tiny, cheaply made shack on a small plot is assessed by the tax collector at a low figure, and consequently, the annual tax collected is small. The builder who erects a fine, well-designed and well-constructed housing project, providing playgrounds and recreation rooms for the tenants, discovers that the homes he provides are assessed at a high figure. Thus, present tax policy rewards the man who constructs a community liability and punishes the man who provides a community asset.

The tax system should encourage, not penalize, housing

---

[1] An unusually fine, well-documented study on the concealed costs of slums was made by the Regional Association of Cleveland and published as "Publication No. 20" in 1948. The report, entitled *Does Good Housing Pay?* was written by Warren P. Phelan. Copies may be obtained from the Regional Association of Cleveland.

developments that supply—without expense to the city
—parks and playgrounds which reduce the need for public recreational facilities paid out of tax funds. Enlightened private builders and owners are entitled to share in
the public saving.

In the case of new buildings, it might be practical to
relate the tax to the amortization period. A well-designed
and well-built dwelling that justifies an amortization period of fifty years should pay a lower tax than a cheap
and undesirable dwelling with a life only half as long.

The feasibility of giving a housing project or a certain
area of the city a special rating, based on its use of city
services, should certainly be explored. Thus an area with
little disease, crime, and fire loss would be accorded a
lower tax rate than an area that was above the city average on those counts. There are ample precedents for this
principle in the insurance field. A healthy individual pays
less for life insurance than the person in poor health. The
fire insurance rate for a concrete and steel building is
much lower than the rate for an old wooden structure.
Many insurance policies make provision for adjustment of
the rate based on actual experience. The principle seems
to have validity when extended to real estate taxes.

Few things are more sacred than long-established tax
customs. Any attempt to change the present system will
arouse bitter opposition. However, thorny as the problem
may be, we must grapple with it if we really are determined to bring down the monthly cost of good housing.

*Tax laws should recognize the obvious fact that well-
built and well-planned housing with a healthful, law-
abiding population means a real saving to the community.*

11

The *cost of housing* and the *cost of a house* are not the same thing. The assumption of their identity is a basic fallacy that makes much discussion of the subject sterile.

The *cost of housing* is made up of three components, none of which is necessarily reduced by lowering construction cost.

The *cost of capital*—first and largest component—may be increased, rather than lowered, by cheapening the construction if the economies shorten the life of the dwelling, thus increasing amortization. Sound construction and adequate space standards, inside and out, will guarantee long, useful life and slow depreciation and will thereby justify both a low rate of interest and low annual amortization.

The second component, *cost of operation,* is generally increased by cheapening construction. Low initial cost usually spells high maintenance and many repair bills.

The *cost of utilities,* especially electric current, a large and neglected factor in *cost,* deserves attention as a promising field for the reduction of the *cost of housing.*

The third component, local *real estate taxes,* bears no relation to the cost of construction. The theory that cheap construction entitles a builder to enjoy a low tax assessment is upside-down economics. Low taxes should be the reward of the community to the developer who provides well-built projects with self-contained recreational areas and self-supported street cleaning. Good housing costs the builder more—but the community less.

12

The new technology which has become predominant in America has not been applied to shelter. From the production standpoint, housing is still archaic. The average American worker produces three times as much—in some fields four times as much—as his European counterpart. Only in the field of housing construction does our technology lag.

Moreover, leading technicians are agreed that the costs of production of housing could be reduced "at least 20% and perhaps as much as 40% by the removal of senseless requirements imposed upon the industry by obsolete local building codes, union rules, mortgage requirements, and other regulations." [1]

They found, also, that "more than a billion dollars a year could be saved by dimensional co-ordination on a

---

[1] This statement was made by a group of experts which included Ralph T. Walker, president of the American Institute of Architects; five residential builders including Clarke Daniel, chairman of the design and construction committee of the National Association of Home Builders; James Price, head of the Prefabricated Home Manufacturers Institute; Walker Lee of the New York State Building Code Commission, Howard Coonley, former president of the American Standards Association, and representatives of the Federal Public Health Service and of research, lumber, brick, iron and steel and electrical industries. The *New York Times*, February 8, 1951.

four-inch module" and that "if bathroom layouts were standardized, prefabricated plumbing assemblies could save millions of pounds of pipe and millions of man-hours," while "excessive street widths imposed on most low-cost developments waste millions of pounds of copper wiring, steel pipe and cement, and millions of man-hours." [1]

13

Here are five practical steps to bring about a reduction in real monthly cost.

1. Legislation should be enacted to make funds for housing available to co-operatives and limited-dividend housing corporations at not more than 3% interest. These loans should be suitably insured to give the lender security. The tenants or buyers should be similarly protected with assurances of sound construction and adequate space.

2. Parallel with action to reduce the interest rates on housing loans, the government should use its efforts to improve the quality of construction and the design of new projects. The goal should be to promote the construction of homes that will justify anticipation of a fifty-year useful life and, simultaneously, to make mortgage loans available on a fifty-year amortization basis.

3. Federal and state governments should initiate studies designed to simplify, modernize, and standardize local

---

[1] *New York Times*, op. cit.

building codes which, in most localities, shackle new construction with archaic regulations.

4. Federal housing agencies should enlist the aid of other agencies, public and private, to investigate the cost of utilities. Is electric current for home use overpriced? The best way to find out would be by constructing a number of pilot plants in housing projects. Their construction on an experimental basis should be encouraged.

5. The tax structure should be re-examined to find a more just measure of taxation than appraised value. A new standard should be sought which would relate local real estate taxes assessed against a home to the cost of the services rendered by the locality to the occupants.

III. *Prefabrication: Hope or Hoax?*

1

THERE are about 30,000 separate parts in the average house.[1] Putting these parts together on the site is an expensive process. Why not cut housing costs by assembling most of the house in a factory? Why not build and market houses the way we build and market automobiles, refrigerators, and washing machines?

It sounds logical enough. Moreover, some of the best industrial brains have pronounced the idea practical as well. In the days when a Chevrolet cost $800, Alfred P. Sloan, Jr. of General Motors estimated that, if the same car were hand-made, it would cost $5000. He said it should be possible to apply factory methods to housing, producing a 5-room dwelling with heating plant and electric stove and

---

[1] "If we count all the items that are ordered in one piece, but exclude separate pieces of assembled parts, as in a lock or medicine cabinet, pieces cut in two on the job, loose items like nails and screws, and plastic materials like plaster, the parts going into a detached house of average size exceed 30,000." *American Housing Problems and Prospects* (New York: Twentieth Century Fund, Inc.; 1944 & 1947), p. 41. Also see: "The Integrated House" *Architectural Forum*, April, 1937, and Peter A. Stone and R. Harold Denton: *Toward More Housing* (Temporary Economic Committee Monograph, No. 8, 1940, pp. 132–133.)

electric washer for around $2500—the equivalent of about $5000 in 1951.

Many experts agreed with Mr. Sloan. Prefabrication, they said, was the solution for an industry still using techniques that were old-fashioned before the horse and buggy came into use.

Prefabrication means different things to different people. A good definition is the one filed with the Department of Commerce in 1947 by the Prefabricated Home Manufacturers' Institute:

"A prefabricated home is one having walls, partitions, floors, ceilings, and/or roof composed of sections or panels varying in size which have been fabricated in a factory prior to erection on the building foundation. This is in contrast to the conventionally built home which is constructed piece by piece on the site."

Prefabrication is by no means a new idea. Burnham Kelly has told how thousands of prefabricated houses were shipped from New York and from Europe, Australia, and Asia to shelter the California gold miners a century ago.[1] During the Civil War there was considerable use of the standardized panel form. In 1892 Ernest F. Hodgson began building small panel dwellings for which he developed a modest but steady market in the New England area. Hodgson's houses were soon in demand as stables, tool houses, and vacation cottages.

Thomas A. Edison was one of the first to experiment with a concrete house. In 1908 he used cast-iron molds to

---

[1] Burnham Kelly: *The Prefabrication of Houses* (Cambridge: The Technology Press; 1951). The author is indebted to the Albert Farwell Bemis Foundation and to Mr. Kelly for permission to use this admirable study as a source of factual information.

pour one- and two-story dwellings. The concrete house proved impractical and Edison abandoned the venture.

2

Interest in prefabricated houses boomed during the depression of the 1930s. Spurred by data showing that 79% of the nation's families could not pay $4000 for a house and lot, designers and manufacturers studied the use of new methods and new materials. Two agencies created under the Roosevelt administration, the Farm Security Agency and the Tennessee Valley Authority, planned and built a number of prefab colonies.

The disparity between the need for new homes and the supply provided by builders was dramatized in the 1930s as never before. During the early years of that decade the unemployed millions included 75% of the workers in the building trades. There was a desperate need for shelter. Yet, nobody had sufficient ingenuity to put the idle labor to work at producing homes. Only a small trickle of new dwellings was actually built. The average annual production from 1930 to 1935 was only 193,000.

By 1939 the shortage of housing in this country was conservatively put at 4 million dwellings. Mass production of housing by factory methods seemed to be the perfect answer.

Several prefabricated houses had made their debut at the Century of Progress Exposition in Chicago in 1933–34.

The slogan of one manufacturer, "Twice as good a house at half the cost," set the pace for a great prefab publicity spree. Newspapers and mass circulation magazines began to vie with each other in imaginative descriptions of the impending housing revolution. An article, typical of the period, in the *Woman's Home Companion* of March, 1935, opened with this paragraph:

"Ann, will you come shopping with me this afternoon? I'm going to buy a house." That is what you may except to hear one woman say to another in the next few weeks as you walk along the street . . . for the packaged house is here and will soon be exhibited in your favorite department store.

One well-publicized house of the period was the Moto-home, produced by Houses Inc., a company backed by the General Electric Company and the American Radiator Company. A cellophane-wrapped model of this flat-roof house with steel frame and asbestos cement panels was unveiled in Wanamaker's department store, New York City, in 1935. The flamboyant claims made for prefabricated housing are typified in this Wanamaker advertisement: "From the chaos of the greatest war and the greatest depression we emerge now into a new age in which American Motohomes are destined to become the most significant symbol of social progress and of economic security."

The call of destiny did not sway all of the estimated half a million persons who inspected the Motohome, "the prefabricated house that comes complete with food in the refrigerator." In fact, fewer than two hundred houses were sold. American Radiator soon gave up its interest and General Electric also withdrew.

The American Radiator Company continued to experiment with prefabrication through its John B. Pierce Foundation. One significant result of this research was the estimate that a small family could be fitted into 672 square feet (24' x 28'), a pattern that has been widely copied by conventional builders as well as prefabricators.[1] Plywood, concrete, cellular glass, and many other materials were tested by the Foundation. In July, 1939, a plywood house was built on an experimental basis in Lebanon, New Jersey, at a cost of a little more than $2000.[2] An experimental family spent a winter in the experimental house. By springtime, the family reported that they had been chilly on every cold day and the Pierce Foundation's experts agreed that thicker walls and better insulation were needed. By then the tentative cost had increased to about $2500. However, engineers never did manage to catch up with the predictions of their publicity men.

3

Up until the Second World War, prefabricated housing accounted for only one-half of one per cent of total housing construction. The war radically changed that figure. The need for large-scale production at minimum cost and maximum speed gave established prefabricators and would-be prefabricators a golden opportunity. The Fed-

---

[1] See pages 87, 95, and 166 for proper standards of size.
[2] *Business Week* reported in September, 1939, that this house could probably be produced in quantity to sell for $1750.

eral Public Housing Authority alone built some 116,000 prefab houses and about 80,000 more were built by other government agencies and by private operators. Prefabricated housing represented 16% of all the dwellings built in 1942.

Encouraged by the tremendous expansion of the industry, the prefabricators and their publicists began to dust off and embellish their grandiose pre-war dreams. At last, they said, the family of modest income would be able to buy a brand new house—once the war was over.

Big industry prepared to convert war plants into house factories. American Rolling Mills and Great Lakes Steel studied the production of prefabricated houses. U. S. Steel bought a controlling interest in Gunnison Homes, a widely publicized prefabricated housing concern. Goodyear Tire and Rubber Company decided it could make a house to sell for about $1800 and officers talked of impending production of tens of thousands of houses. A feature story in the *Saturday Evening Post* of October 21, 1944, described what was to come: "In the future, housebuilding seems likely to become as prolific as in the past were those industries producing automobiles, refrigerators, radios, and washing machines. Goodyear is going to build houses because its management is persuaded the corporation can make money manufacturing and selling homes."

Catering to the American demand for speed, prefab publicity hammered away at the dawn-to-dusk erection schedule. Newspapers and magazines published hundreds of photographs of walls being raised by gangs of workmen, roofs being lowered by portable cranes. *Life* showed in pictures how a prefab was erected in fifty-eight minutes in Texas in 1941; four years later the same magazine reported a thirty-four minute job in California, but the *Christian Science Monitor* had already eclipsed this with the story of a twenty-minute house. There was reason to hope—or fear—that the four-minute house would be next.

People who get tired of living in one speed-record home could easily switch to another, the public was assured. A writer for *Collier's* forecast in 1943: "When your home of tomorrow gets old and battered and out of date you will not have to sell it and move away. You will merely turn it in for a new one with all the latest improvements. Built-in furniture, lightweight material, and standardized shapes will make the small houses of the future as simple to re-place as automobiles and gas stoves. . . . The cost of the exchange will probably not exceed a thousand dollars." [1]

And where would the new home be turned in and ex-changed for the new model? At a local department store or other retail outlet. In fact, there might even be used-house lots for the very lowest income people!

During the war, one prefabricated housing concern, the Homasote Company, received immense acclaim and news-paper headlines by speedily erecting 5000 houses for the Navy at Portsmouth, Virginia. The Homasote house was made of wallboard manufactured out of repulped waste paper.

On the basis of Homasote's publicity, which consumed

------

[1] In 1944, when the belief was general that all housing problems would soon be solved by the miracles of prefabrication, the author wrote: "No belief is more unjustified, no misconception is the source of more confusion than the myth that an impending revolution in building tech-niques gives promise of enabling private enterprise to provide healthful housing within the means of the people who live in the slums." From: *The Seven Myths of Housing* (New York: Alfred A. Knopf; 1944), p. 117.

almost enough pulp to build a small housing project, Macy's department store in New York was induced to handle the sale of Homasote houses. Although the price was far beyond earlier forecasts, $13,500, some fifty customers placed orders. But the manufacturer was apparently unable to produce even at this price, for, so far as can be ascertained, not one house was ever delivered to a Macy customer. This experience is typical of a pattern repeated over and over again in dozens of communities throughout the country.

4

A dramatic chapter in the story of prefabrication was written just after the end of World War II. It was ushered in with a roll of drums as Housing Expediter, Wilson W. Wyatt, early in 1946, issued a ukase. He announced that the prefabrication housing industry, with his assistance, must produce 250,000 prefabs in 1946 and 600,000 in 1947. The National Housing Agency would offer priority ratings so prefabricators could get scarce materials. As a further inducement the Federal government offered to buy at cost any dwellings that a manufacturer was unable to sell.

When the industry had sufficiently recovered from the shock of this amazing proclamation, scores of prefabricators and would-be prefabricators began to make plans for covering the land with factory-made houses. *Fortune* said,

in April, 1946, that the industry thought it could meet
Wyatt's goal if the government would provide enough plywood, gypsum board, and other materials. The magazine
continued: "Like gophers after a windstorm, 'prefabricators' began popping up in February when Wilson Wyatt
announced that the government was preparing to stimulate production of some 250,000 prefabricated houses this
year and 600,000 in 1947. At once R. G. Le Tourneau, the
earth mover, unveiled a massive contraption that would
roll to a house site, pour a complete house, let it set for
twenty-four hours, then rumble on to a new site. A company in Los Angeles was said to be ready to provide
habitable igloos by spraying concrete over an inflated rubber hemisphere that could be deflated and carried out the
front door once the concrete had set. Everybody talked
about the steel house and the aluminum house. And Henry
Kaiser, never daunted, was reported ready to make houses
with or without lumber, with or without brick, with or
without steel."

Priority ratings were obtained by some 280 producers or
prospective producers. The long heralded prefab boom
was apparently under way.

5

The prefabricated housing industry did not produce
250,000 houses in 1946 or 600,000 in 1947. Production
since the war has been:

	PREFABS	PER CENT OF ALL DETACHED HOUSES
1946	37,200	6.9
1947	37,400	5.1
1948	30,000	3.9
1949	35,000	4.1
1950	55,000	4.8

What went wrong? Why has the prefabrication industry produced only about 5% of the single-family houses since the war, compared to 16% of the single-family houses produced in 1942?

Various excuses were put forward by the industry, such as shortage of materials, opposition from certain real estate interests, etc. However, these were not the real reasons for the failure to fulfill the predictions of its enthusiastic advocates.[1]

There is no doubt but that prefabrication is more efficient, more saving of labor and materials, than conventional methods of building. A Congressional committee found that a machine-made prefab house requires an average of only five hundred man-hours in the factory and on the site, as against 1500 to 2500 hours at the site for a conventional dwelling.[2]

The Congressional subcommittee supplies the answer: "Three-fifths of the cost of a prefabricated house is often added after it leaves the factory. One prefabricator, for

---

[1] In April 1951, the president of the Prefabricated Home Manufacturers Institute, John C. Taylor, Jr., predicted that the industry would build one out of every five homes in 1955. The mass market for prefabricated homes, he declared, will be for one containing 950 to 1000 square feet and priced at no more than $10,000, including land cost. *New York Times,* April 29, 1951.

[2] 80th Congress, 1st Session, *Report of a Subcommittee of the Joint Committee on Housing.*

example, sold a home f.o.b. factory for a little over $3,000 and later received total cost figures on it of more than $10,000. Plumbing contractors' charges vary widely, often ranging from $360 to $650 on identical models erected in different towns. . . .

"Over-enthusiastic proponents of prefabrication have frequently promised revolutionary results in cost reduction—results which could be attained only by readjusting overnight the whole building industry to create a utopian setting for prefabrication."

The Congressional committee's judgment is supported by responsible spokesmen for the industry who point out that a prefab house which is advertised and sold f.o.b. factory for $2500 may cost the buyer nearly $7000 by the time he moves in.

The real reason why the prefabricators cannot produce a low-cost dwelling is, of course, that the shell of the house, the part which is affected by prefabrication, accounts for less than 40% of the price of the completed house.[1] Thus some 60% of the price the purchaser will have to pay before he moves into the new home is concealed at the time he buys it at the factory.

Factory production of the shell does not reduce the cost of the land, the foundation, grading, landscaping, and similar items. It does not reduce the cost of wiring and utility connections. Moreover, prefabrication of the shell does not touch such items as the sink, the range, kitchen cabinets, the refrigerator, or plumbing equipment and fixtures.

According to John J. O'Brien, president of Gunnison Homes, a United States Steel Corporation subsidiary and

---

[1] See Chapter X—*British Housing Policies* by Eric L. Bird.

one of the large prefabricators, "approximately one hundred per cent of the package price paid to Gunnison Homes, Inc., should be added to complete the house for occupancy. This would include freight, all construction costs to two feet outside the house, and the dealer's profit." [1]

National Homes Corporation, Lafayette, Indiana, believed to be the largest producer of prefabricated homes, confirms that "the factory price represents roughly one-half of the final sales price of the house, *exclusive of land*." [2]

"The great attraction of the manufactured house is the promise not only of efficiency but of cheapness, due to the competitive production of houses in large quantities. It is doubtful if this will prove to be a great element in reducing the cost of housing. The reason is simple. The shell of the building is not the largest element in the cost. . . . The two spots where mass production would take the place of present methods, namely in the shell itself, and in the assemblage of parts, offer only a minor field for reduction. To cut the cost of the shell in half is to lower the cost of the house a bare 10 per cent." [3]

---

[1] Letter to the author dated June 23, 1950.

[2] Letter from James R. Price, president of the corporation, to the author dated June 29, 1950.

[3] Lewis Mumford: *City Development* (New York: Harcourt, Brace and Company; 1945), pp. 69–70.

6

From a peak variously estimated at two hundred to four hundred in 1946, the number of prefab producers shrank to about 130 by 1947 and to about 85 by 1949. The decline in the number of manufacturers was a sign of health rather than an omen of doom. Scores of under-capitalized and ill-equipped companies disappeared from the scene. Their exit has not weakened the industry.

The seven largest companies accounted for about 38% of the 35,000 houses produced in 1949.[1]

Only one of these companies, Gunnison Homes, is owned by a corporation giant (U. S. Steel). The great corporations apparently have lost their zest for tackling the thorny problems of prefabrication.

The median number of shipments for 85 producers in 1949 was 200 houses. The smallest firms shipped as few as 25. Many of the small companies seemed happy to remain small, serving their immediate area and avoiding the headaches involved in establishing branch factories

---

[1] Listed in approximate order of size (figures on production are seldom revealed) they were:

National Homes Corporation, Lafayette, Indiana
American Houses Inc., New York, New York
Lumber Fabricators, Detroit, Michigan
Crawford Corporation, Baton Rouge, Louisiana
Gunnison Homes Inc., New Albany, Indiana
Pease Woodwork Company, Cincinnati, Ohio
Harnischfeger Corporation, Port Washington, Wisconsin

and a system of national distribution. Indeed, National Homes Corporation limits its sales to a 300-mile radius, although most of the other big companies welcome customers anywhere.

7

Contrary to the general notion that a prefabricated house is fundamentally a different kind of house, most of the prefab companies produce the traditional wood frame structure with shop-built panels of studs, insulation, and sheathing. The panels are either room-size or modular— i.e., in sizes that are multiples of a common denominator, usually four. Materials for the floors, ceilings, and roofs are generally precut. Assembled on the site, this house is hardly distinguishable from houses built by conventional methods. And there is no distinguishable difference in price.

Technically superior to this prefab is the one made of panels in which plywood is bonded to the studs with glue and nails. This is known as "stressed-skin" construction. One manufacturer, Harnischfeger Corporation, claims that its stressed-skin walls are up to fourteen times stronger than ordinary walls and that their five-ply subfloor eliminates squeaks. About one-third of all the prefabricated houses marketed today are built of some type of plywood.

Measured by the lung power of its promoters and the columns of newspaper space given to its praises, the most promising kind of prefab was the metal house. The adjective "promising" is used deliberately, for the metal prefabricated house was 99% promise and only 1% performance.

Buckminster Fuller's *Dymaxion* house, first projected in 1927, was a classic example. The house was to be hexagonal, suspended by wires from a central mast somewhat like a merry-go-round. Aluminum and other light-weight materials would provide the maximum area per pound. The *Dymaxion* house was one of the most visited exhibits at the Chicago Century of Progress in 1933–34. It is doubtful if the Wright brothers' pioneer flight at Kitty Hawk claimed as many inches of newspaper and magazine space as were given by editors to the *Dymaxion* house in the years after its debut. However, so far as the author has been able to determine, no family in America has ever lived in a *Dymaxion* house.

On the west coast, Southern California Homes has actually produced a number of houses assembled from light-weight panels consisting of a honeycomb paper core surfaced with thin-gauge aluminum sheets. General Homes has marketed an aluminum house.

The most publicized metal house was the enameled steel product of Lustron Corporation. With invested capital of only $36,000 and with similarly little demonstrated ability to build housing, the Lustron Corporation in 1947 obtained a loan of $37.5 million from the Reconstruction Finance Corporation. This strange loan of more than one thousand times the invested capital of the borrowing corporation did not produce many houses, but it did produce acres of newspaper and magazine publicity. The company immediately "predicted" that it would manufacture 120,-

000 in 1948.[1] However, in that year it produced only a few dozen. By January, 1950, the company had actually completed 2096 houses.

Some of Lustron's production forecasts were:

January 1947	100 houses a day by September 1947
November 1947	30,000 a year within nine months
April 1948	125 a day by mid-June
October 1948	150 a day by summer
February 1949	150 a day by summer
January 1950	1149 a month by July

For the last nine months of 1949, when production was greatest, the company turned out an average of six houses a day.

The final chapter of the Lustron Corporation fiasco was the sale, on the auction block June 6, 1950, of its assets in an attempt by the government to recover some of the $37.5 million loaned the corporation. Every Lustron house thus will have *cost the American taxpayer* more than $17,000.

8

The prefabrication industry seems at last to have come to the realization that the public is weary of boastful prophecies. The feature story describing a new technique of prefabrication that "promises to do for the home-

---

[1] Arthur Bartlett, "Lustron—the House That Lots of Jack Built," *Collier's*, November 5, 1949.

building industry what Henry Ford did for the automobile industry"—a hardy perennial of the Sunday supplements for at least a decade—has disappeared.

Prefabrication has, however, certain inherent advantages over conventional methods of construction which cannot be dismissed as unimportant. In the first place, people who care about the engineering of their homes are impressed by the structural soundness of the best of the prefabricated houses, often superior to the product of the average speculative builder. Speed of erection is another characteristic superiority of the prefabricated house. A third advantage is, perhaps, greater certainty, in advance, of the total cost of the completed house, avoiding some of the uncertainties and the "extras" that plague the man who builds a home by conventional methods.

Despite these advantages, the industry is hampered by obstacles which it has yet to surmount.

The chief of these are:

1. *Financing.* Many banks are still reluctant to lend on prefabs and FHA has blown hot or cold depending on locality. Nearly half of the 31 prefabricators reporting to the Prefabricated Home Manufacturers' Institute in 1949 said "conflicting FHA requirements in various areas" had limited their production. Moreover, the manufacturer needs his money when the house is shipped but the dealer does not want to pay until he sells and collects. A method of interim financing is badly needed.

2. *Public scepticism.* Many potential buyers still think a prefab house must be either the dreary type of dwelling produced for war workers, or something as radical as Fuller's *Dymaxion* house. The misleading publicity campaigns in which the industry has indulged in the past have

made prospective customers sceptical about modest and truthful claims. One postwar survey showed that only 17% of the potential buyers would consider a prefab. If the industry is to overcome this resistance, sustained programs of education through truthful advertising must be launched.

Prefabricators spend about $1 per $7000 house for advertising; in contrast, the automobile industry spends about $45 to sell $7000 worth of cars.[1]

3. *Building codes.* There are about 2000 different state and local building codes in the United States. Most of these codes specify the *kinds* and *dimensions* of materials instead of setting standards for performance. For instance, a 2″ x 4″ stud wall will be specified, although plywood construction with 2″ x 3″ studs may be considerably stronger than 2″ x 4″ lumber to which the code was originally intended to apply. The procedure necessary to get deviations from the local building code approved by the local supervisory board or commission is often so cumbersome that the manufacturer gives up.

4. *Transportation costs.* Much of the money saved in factory construction can be eaten up by transportation. The Joint Committee on Housing reported that when conventional building materials are used the practical range of the market is 200 to 300 miles from the factory. One manufacturer has reckoned that house cost increases at the rate of fifty cents a truck mile per hundred pounds from plant to site.

5. *Labor opposition.* Although most of the larger prefab plants have been unionized, opposition by AFL building trades workers has persisted in some localities. This hos-

---

[1] Burnham Kelly: *The Prefabrication of Houses,* op. cit.

tility has discouraged manufacturers from providing panels finished to the last possible degree—with a resultant increase in the cost of labor on the site of erection.

6. *Opposition by building material jobbers.* Since the manufacturer of a prefabricated house sells direct to a local dealer, the building material jobber is frozen out. The jobber or dealer in building materials has long been an institution in the industry. Even large manufacturers of building supplies and plumbing and heating equipment have been unwilling to sell direct to builders. When prefabricators short circuit the jobber, the latter's natural resentment is directed toward the builder who is often the local agent for the prefabricated house. Since many builders are dependent upon the local jobber for credit when they build conventionally, the jobber is in a position to make his opposition to prefabricated housing effective.

7. *Geographical requirements.* The brunette secretary in New Orleans needs the same kind of typewriter used by her blond counterpart in New York. The head of a family of four uses the same size automobile as a bachelor. However, housing needs vary in different climates and for families of different sizes. Makers of typewriters can concentrate on one machine. Automobile manufacturers can standardize on 2 or 3 basic models. But a prefabricator of homes has a market of widely varying tastes and needs. In an effort to suit everybody he is tempted to make so many styles and sizes that the economies of mass production are lost.

All of these obstacles might and undoubtedly will be surmounted. The fundamental weakness will still remain. *Prefabrication has failed as a means of reducing the cost of housing because it concentrates on the shell of the house which represents less than half the cost of the structure and, of course, a much smaller proportion of the monthly cost of housing.*

9

The dream of a prefabricated house wrapped in cellophane, bought at the department store, delivered and erected in one day, is over. But that is no reason to write off the possibility that American ingenuity may yet solve the problems involved in a real reduction in housing costs.

The first step in this, as in any other attack on housing costs, is to recognize the fact that many things are involved of which the cost of the shell of the house is only one. Hope of success lies in extending the mass production principle to every aspect of housing. This will require financial resources and technical skills that can be provided only by great building companies, equipped to deal with every aspect of home production. Above all, it will involve bold imagination.

An industrial corporation determined to make an all-out attack on housing costs would start with problems of financing so as to obtain long-term loans at minimum interest rates. The corporation would proceed to explore methods of acquiring, processing, and landscaping sites so as to achieve the most advantageous use. Research projects would be set up for the study of labor relations, of building codes, of the relation of real estate taxes to the value of the services rendered by the municipality. A technical division would explore measures to reduce the cost of gas and electricity for household use.

It might prove more important thus to discover means of increasing the life of the house by ten years than to reduce by 10% the construction cost. It might have a greater effect on the "rent" to cut the cost of electric current in half than to cut the cost of the walls of the house in half. To reduce the interest rate on housing funds would certainly be a greater contribution toward reduction of the cost of housing than such economies as eliminating storage space or reducing the size of rooms.[1]

While this technique is not "prefabrication" in its generally understood sense, it is a method of attack that gives hope of success in overcoming difficulties with which the construction industry has wrestled in vain. *The technique is, in essence, the application of fundamental mass production economics to shelter.*

The achievements of every American industry, from railroads to aviation and television, have been based upon what has been learned from the failures of the past. There is good reason to believe that the home production industry, aided by government, will yet build upon past failures to achieve success in reducing real housing costs.

---

[1] The Levitt & Sons, Inc., organization operating on Long Island, New York, has shown the effectiveness of this approach.

IV. *Home Ownership: Pro and Con*

1

THROUGHOUT the ages man has dreamed of a roof, four walls, and a plot of ground that he could call his very own. To establish a home, where generation after generation might be born, live, and die, was to perform a hallowed rite. Only within the last few decades has the pattern of our civilization so changed as to make this traditional attitude toward home ownership unsuited to the realities of life.

If there is one characteristic that distinguishes our society from all that has gone before, it is greater mobility. People move more easily, more frequently.

The young insurance salesman who buys a house in the Chicago suburbs may be transferred to the branch in San Francisco. The sheet metal worker may find himself jobless in New York City when there is a demand for men skilled in his trade to work on air conditioning equipment in Houston. Textile workers in New England towns have been left stranded when factories moved south. Southern laborers have been forced to migrate to the north and west

in search of employment. In all walks of life people move
from place to place, impelled by economic pressures.

Stability and immobility, the very characteristics which
endeared home ownership to earlier generations, are its
greatest drawbacks today.

2

_____

For a family in the upper-income brackets purchase of
a house is often a wise use of funds. For a middle-income
family it may be a good investment, too, if the purchase is
made during a time of economic depression, when houses
—and nearly everything else—are offered for sale at bargain prices. For a family in the lower-income half, however, the step is rarely to be recommended and is dangerous if the purchase is made at a high price in a period
of economic prosperity. Yet that is the very time when
most families feel the urge to buy. Good business, high
wages, and housing shortages go together and exert pressures that induce home seekers to sign a contract and
make a down payment on a house. Thus, most people buy
when the market is high and sell when prices fall.[1]

The dream of home ownership is human and commendable. Those who share it must understand, however,
that the average low-income American family cannot ful-

_____

[1] Home ownership in the United States rose 71% between 1940 and
1950, "the largest increase for any decade on record," bringing total
home ownership up to 19.5 million families as compared with 17.1 million rent-paying families. These figures are from a 1951 report of the
Housing and Home Finance Agency.

fill the dream except at grave risk to its own economic security.

Fortunately, some of the pleasure in personal possession which once was centered in the home, may be found today in ownership of a radio-phonograph, a television set, or an automobile. Modern man can and should have possessions which are partial substitutes for the emotional satisfaction of home ownership. Unlike the traditional family home, these beloved substitutes are not anchored to the ground. They can go along with the family wherever opportunity or destiny may beckon.

3

A few years ago the author was invited to give a talk on housing to veterans at a convalescent hospital. A warm welcome, evidenced by resounding applause, greeted him as he entered the hall. Here, the men evidently felt, is someone who can tell us the best way to buy a house when we are discharged from the hospital and returned to civilian life.

Instead, the speaker gave a realistic picture of home ownership. He tried to discourage the veterans from buying a house before they were sure where they would settle down and how much they could earn. Finally, he warned that the man who bought in the high-priced postwar market and fettered himself with exorbitant monthly payments for twenty-five years might come to feel that he did not own the house, but instead, that the house owned him.

At the conclusion of the talk, as the speaker walked down the aisle to the door at the back of the hall, the only sound was the clicking of his footsteps on the wooden floor. The veterans who would have applauded the conventional cliches about the dream of every American family were numbed into hurt silence by the plain truth.

What were the unpleasant facts that so disturbed those men? Let us see what happened to one of them after his return to civilian life. We will call him Ted Brown. He and his wife, Peggy, have one child. At present, they are living doubled up with Peggy's parents. But they dream of the day when they will have a home of their own.

Ted has a job, not as good as some, but better than many. He earns $60 a week, an average income for the employed factory or office worker. So far as any wage earner can be said to be typical, he can claim that distinction. Ted's job is steady. He has no special reason to fear unemployment.

Peggy feels that they have been living with her parents much too long, yet she insists realistically that any plans for a home of their own must be based on that $60 paycheck, not on rosy hopes for the future.

So the Browns start to read the real estate pages in the Sunday newspapers. They find many advertisements of houses for sale, but they have decided that they do not want to buy. It will be easier to maintain a budget, they feel, if there is a fixed amount due each month as rent. Peggy says, "What do we know about the cost of keeping up a house? If we rent, we can be sure of the cost and we can manage within our income."

Ted is not so set against buying. He is still young and

confident of his own ability to overcome any obstacle. He would be willing to take a chance—but he agrees to look for rental housing first.

The Browns know the sound old rule of thumb that a family should not spend more than a week's income for a month's rent. But they soon make the disconcerting discovery that there is no apartment or house advertised at a price which fits their budget, $60 a month. They want a minimum of three rooms and prefer four—two bedrooms, a living room with a dining alcove, kitchen, and bath. The advertisements describe this as "four-and-a-half rooms." The only housing offered at the rent they can afford is one-room and two-room apartments in rundown neighborhoods.

Ted begins to feel frustrated. And he boils over as his eye catches a full page advertisement in a Sunday newspaper, illustrated with a drawing of the Statue of Liberty.

"Listen to this one, Peggy: 'For generations, the Statue of Liberty has greeted newcomers to the United States of America as a symbol of our basic freedom, which has made possible the American way of life. And now a new community at the entrance of New York harbor symbolizes this American way. Shore-Haven is a new monument to the American spirit of free enterprise. The project was conceived, planned, executed by Fred C. Trump, acting as a free and rugged individualist to meet the basic need for shelter. . . . And now, for generations to come, hundreds of American families will live happily in this newly created garden apartment centre, making it a living monument to the American Way of Life.'" [1]

---

[1] From an advertisement of "Fred C. Trump, Builder," which appeared in *The New York Times* on January 16, 1949.

"How lovely!" says Peggy. "I'd adore living in a monument. But can we afford it?"

"Wait a minute, let me finish. 'Three-and-a-half rooms, $105.' Why, I'd have to get a raise of about $40 to be able to live there!" Ted throws the paper on the floor in disgust.

As a matter of fact, a family should have at least $5000 a year to pay the rent quoted. Only one family out of four has that much income. Although Ted Brown may not understand much of economics, he does sense the hypocrisy of advertising homes that are beyond the means of three-quarters of the population as "monuments to the American way of life." [1]

4

Ted and Peggy continue their search a few weeks longer —without result. They scan all the real estate ads and they talk with real estate agents. Nobody offers to rent a decent four-room apartment for $60. Wearily Ted sums up the problem: "I know you don't *want* to buy a house, Peggy. Neither do I. But we'll have to—unless you want to stay here with your parents the rest of our lives. I don't!"

So the Browns turn to the advertisements of houses for sale. Ted finds this:

"The irresistible ranch home that set Long Island buzzing with excitement. Set in a spacious, carefully planned community, this ranch sensation is an architect's dream

---

[1] Fewer than 10% of all families in the country paid more than $100 a month rent in 1951.

come true. Automatic kitchen, fluorescent lighting, two
walls of baked enamel cabinets, colored tile bath with
sun-ray lamp, oil burner radiant heat, near railroad, bus
at door. No cash for vets." [1]

"How much?" asks Peggy.

"Only $68 a month 'for everything,' the ad says.

"Wait a minute. Does that $68 really cover everything,
the same as rent?"

"Of course, it does," Ted replies impatiently. "And don't
tell me it isn't true, because it says 'FHA approved' right
in the ad. That means the Federal Housing Administration, Uncle Sam, is backing what they say. But here's one
for only $59 in a place called Coronet Homes.[2] We'd get a
'pine paneled dining room, electric kitchen, Hollywood
bath, a picture window and easy terms.' "

Peggy is unconvinced. She begs Ted to curb his im-
patience. Reluctantly he assents—at least to wait a while
longer. Yet, he cannot help stealing a look at the real estate
pages where, week after week, he sees advertisements describing new houses for sale at monthly costs that are little
more than the $60 he can afford. Glowing adjectives and
purple prose embellish the descriptions and there is always the assurance that the monthly cost named "pays
all."

Finally, after months of chafing at the delay, Ted can
stand it no longer.

"See here, Peggy, here's an ad that spells it all out. It
says, 'You get so much for so little. Six large rooms, huge
panoramic window in living room. Gleaming white cus-

---

[1] From an advertisement for *Miller Homes* which appeared in *The
New York Times*, September 11, 1949.

[2] From an advertisement for *Coronet Homes* which appeared in *The
New York Times*, September 11, 1949.

Only one price tag is shown to the customer—
but both must be paid.

tom-built kitchen cabinets. Attached garage with over-head doors. $72.60 a month like rent pays all.'[1] Now will you believe me when I tell you that we aren't taking any chances if we buy this home. Sure, it's $12.60 a month more than we ought to pay. But it will be our *own home*. I should get a $10 raise soon, anyway."

[1] From an advertisement for *Mayfair Ranch Homes* in the New York *Daily News,* June 10, 1950.

Peggy is at last half-convinced by the statement that the sum named "like rent pays all." She longs for privacy, away from relatives, and she is ready to believe almost anything that will help her to take the step.

The Browns start out for Mayfair Ranch Homes, along with hundreds of other house-hungry couples. Their urgent emotional yearning for four walls of their own will make them easy prey for the high-pressure salesmanship of a glib real estate agent trained in painting a glowing picture to snare just such inexperienced young people.

It never occurs to the Browns to ask the fundamental question: "How many square feet of area in this house?" Moreover, they would not know how to evaluate the reply intelligently, were they to ask. Nobody ever told them that, if the price asked for a house works out at more than $12 per square foot, it can be justified only by unusually sturdy construction which promises low maintenance cost and long useful life.

The Browns ask very few questions. Instead, they do what more than eleven million other families have done in the last decade: they buy a house—not on comparative values, but on comparative adjectives.

5

What do they then discover?

The first jolt comes when they have to pay about $300 in "closing charges" to get their mortgage. This payment covers the closing fee, the FHA application fee, the charge for a credit report, and taxes and insurance in advance for the year ahead.

After they move in, the monthly bill from the local utility company for gas and electricity amounts to $6; there is also a bill of $2 for water and another of $1.50 for garbage collection. Gas, electricity, water, and garbage collection cost them $9.50. Of course, the next month there are the same three bills and there is an added bill of $120 for a winter's supply of oil for heating and hot water.

Ted points out that the cost of fuel is a one-time bill, but Peggy notes that $120 a year means $10 extra a month. The new house is costing, not $72.60 a month, but $72.60 plus $9.50 plus $10, or $92.10.

They do not yet know the whole story. Other even more unexpected items of expense await them in the months ahead. There is an item of $150 for storm windows, and, in the spring, $40 for screens.

Peggy keeps a careful record of the household expenditures. At the end of the first year in the new house she finds they have spent $336 on storm windows, screens, garbage can, grass seed, fertilizer, lawnmower, hose, tools, shrubs, and minor repairs done by outside mechanics. This was an average of $28 a month, bringing their monthly cost to more than $120.

"Of course," says Ted, "we won't have to buy storm windows and garden tools again."

"That's so," replies Peggy, "but we are always going to be spending something extra."

Peggy is right. A handy fellow with tools, Ted is able to fix the small things that go wrong in any house over the years—and especially in cheaply built ones. But a leaking roof or a troublesome oil-burner require mechanics from outside. When the faucet in the sink won't stop dripping, Ted must telephone the plumber to send someone over to repair it. *As owner, Ted gets bills that he never thought of or heard of when he was a tenant.*

Painting, repairs, replacements, and other items will average close to $100 a year, or $8 a month, over a ten-year period. So, disregarding the extra first-year expenses for getting established, this is how the average month's bills will look to the Browns:

Interest and Amortization of mortgage, taxes, and fire insurance	$72.60
Water	2.00
Garbage disposal	1.50
Gas and electricity	6.00
Oil for heating	10.00
Upkeep and Repairs	8.00
TOTAL	$100.10

The true monthly cost of the Browns' house becomes, not the advertised $72.60, but at least $100. There may be still other unforeseen expenses such as the cost of a commutation ticket, if the Browns' new home is located, as are most houses of its kind, in the suburbs.

Like hundreds of other young couples, the Browns find out too late that "$72.60 like rent pays all" is, in the words of Theodore Roosevelt, "a falsehood better called by a shorter and uglier word."

Yet payments on the house must be kept up. The monthly bills for interest and amortization of the mortgage, taxes, and fire insurance (the $72.60 that was going to "pay all") must be met. Bills for gas and electricity arrive regularly every month. Repairs cannot be indefinitely postponed. Year after year, in sickness and in health, in good times and bad, whether Ted has a job or not, the house exacts its regular payments. Ted and Peggy may come to feel that they are chained to a treadmill.

6

Ted may hear of a better job in another city. Of course, if he were living in rented quarters, it would be easy to move. But the house, which he proudly says he "owns" keeps him tied to one spot. As Robert R. Young, chairman of the board of the Chesapeake & Ohio Railway Company, has well said: "Don't buy a house when you are young. It may anchor you to one town and one job."

If hard times come, Ted may find it absolutely essential to move. The curtailing or closing of his plant's operations may cost him his job, and leave him in competition with many other unemployed workers for the few available jobs in the community. Ted may then decide that he *must* move to another town to find work. But the very circumstances that make it necessary for him to pull up stakes and seek his fortune elsewhere will, in all probability, similarly affect other home owners in the same community.

When many want to sell and few want to buy, the price of any commodity falls. Houses are no exception to this economic law. If Ted must sell his house because of a general depression or local unemployment, the price that he will realize will mean a loss of much if not all that he has previously invested in it. If he is unable to sell at any price, the mortgage will be foreclosed, with about the same result so far as Ted and Peggy are concerned.

This aspect of a mortgaged home becomes even more dangerous for the family that buys a home on a farm. A city dweller can continue to operate his gas station or his drug store even if the mortgage on his house is foreclosed. He can keep his job, even if he loses his home. The average farmer cannot. The city dweller may decide, in time of stress, to sacrifice his house to save his business. The farmer is offered no such choice. The same mortgage covers the house and the farm, his home and his business. If he loses his home by foreclosure, he loses his means of livelihood as well.

"Between 1926 and 1938 foreclosures came unpleasantly close to balancing the number of homes built. How many families, buying at today's inflated prices are headed for disaster?" [1]

According to Thomas G. Grace, state director of the Federal Housing Administration: "It is economically impossible for a veteran earning less than $75 to $100 a week to afford the purchase of a home running from $7000 to $10,000. . . . On the 25-year plan, it means that he will have to lay out $65 or more each month for a quarter of a century. That's a long time to be tied down, especially when there is a growing family to consider. And the worst of it is that many of these homes are not reliable structures—they may not be much to look at or live in after half that time." [2]

---

[1] John P. Dean: "Folklore and Taboos" in *The Nation*, May 15, 1948.
[2] Quoted in the *New York World-Telegram* of September 30, 1946.

7

One thing cannot be emphasized too strongly. The real estate speculator's practice of deceiving house buyers with the statement that the monthly carrying charge for interest, amortization, insurance, and taxes "covers everything" leads to disillusionment and grief. The specious half-truth of this claim is dramatically underscored by a comparison with advertising that tells the whole truth about real costs.

A brochure published by *Queensview*, a nonprofit cooperative housing project in New York City for moderate income families, sponsored in 1950–51 by a distinguished group of citizens,[1] reads as follows:

"Monthly carrying charges (in place of rent) will cover *gas* and *electricity, heat* and *hot water*, all *repairs, reserves,* insurance, interest and amortization of the mortgage, real estate taxes and an *adequate contingency fund. Redecoration and replacement of ranges and refrigerators are not contemplated unless revenues permit.*"

The items in italics (supplied) are those omitted from the figure that is supposed to "cover everything" in most newspaper advertisements.

For example, a development in River Edge, New Jersey, called "Continental Ridge" advertised: "The two-bedroom

---

[1] The group included Gerard Swope, chairman; Louis H. Pink, president; Mrs. Mary K. Simkhovitch, Henry Morgenthau Jr., the Very Reverend E. Roberts Moore, David Sarnoff.

home is only $11,990. Veterans pay no cash down, and the $83 monthly charges cover everything." [1] The "Continental Ridge" house is priced about the same as the comparable 4½-room apartment in Queensview, which is valued at $12,100.

Here is a parallel of comparative monthly cost.

	QUEENSVIEW	CONTINENTAL RIDGE
Interest and amortization	$42.50	$66.00
Insurance	1.15	2.00
Taxes	1.00 [2]	15.00
		$83.00
Utilities (gas, electricity, heat and water)	8.40	?
Maintenance and repairs	17.50	?
Reserve for contingencies	5.90	?
TOTAL	$76.45	?

A man who has bought a home in Continental Ridge and lives in it supplies the information that his utility bills average $24 a month: $10 for gas and electricity, $12 for fuel oil, and $2 for water. This raises the $83 monthly charges supposed to "cover everything" to $107—without any allowance for maintenance and repairs. This man estimates that the true monthly cost is about $120—or about 50% more than the advertised figure.

---

[1] *New York Herald Tribune,* June 18, 1950. The Continental Ridge advertisement also fails to mention that all purchasers, including veterans, are required to pay so-called "closing charges" in connection with the mortgage. Closing charges amount to more than $300.

[2] The low figure is explained by partial tax exemption for this cooperative, nonprofit development.

8

The shoddy structures, erected by speculative builders to be unloaded as fast as possible on gullible buyers, will be obsolete in fifteen or twenty years. Meanwhile, the monthly cost to the occupant is high. The cost to the community, in the long run, is likewise high.

Stuart Chase has written of "the incredible, fantastic jerry-built wilderness out beyond Jamaica" [1] in describing conditions around New York. But it is not necessary to single out New York City or the very worst housing developments to see the faults of the present system. For instance, in 1951 a Los Angeles private builder, Fritz Burns, boasted of having produced houses for $5000. Investigation disclosed that these dwellings had an area of only 480 square feet compared with the 575 square feet which the Los Angeles Housing Authority requires as a minimum in its public housing program. Moreover, the buildings containing these tiny apartments are jerry-built with rough pine outside stairways similar to emergency war housing construction. Such shacks are the slums of a decade hence. [2]

Every city in the nation has a large quota of flimsy little houses—many built outside the zone of fire restrictions to escape limitations on poor construction. The floor area is

---

[1] Stuart Chase: "The Case Against Home Ownership" in *Survey Graphic*, May, 1938, p. 263.
[2] See the author's letter to *The Wall Street Journal*, July 30, 1951, p. 4.

often as little as 450 or even 400 square feet.[1] There is no thought of gracious living or provision for recreational facilities. Such ugly and crowded housing developments are covering the suburbs of many cities like a rash—a rash that will not be eradicated for many painful decades.

Minimum space standards for health and decency, according to the committee on hygiene of housing of the American Public Health Association, should be: 450 square feet for one person living alone, 750 square feet for a couple, 1000 square feet for a family of three, 1150 square feet for a family of four, 1400 feet for five, and 1550 for six. Very little of the housing erected since World War II meets those standards. Instead, quoting Dr. C.-E. A. Winslow, chairman of the committee: "In most of our mushrooming suburban housing developments today you cannot tell the house from the garage. If we progress much further in this direction, you won't be able to tell the house from the letter box."[2]

Where does the responsibility lie? Ordinary human greed is partly to blame, of course, but the chief blame must be placed on administrative policies of the Federal Housing Administration. Its "economy house" program is encircling the cities with blotches of shoddy little boxes

---

[1] A news item, which sheds considerable light on the attitude of most speculative builders, read as follows: "The Long Island Home Builders Institute has been authorized by its board of directors to start immediate legal action to set aside the recent order of the Town Board of Babylon, which increased the minimum habitable floor area of homes from 400 to 800 square feet. The executive secretary of the Institute said that '. . . the determination of the size of homes is an improper use of the police powers of the state . . . and has no relation to the safety, health, morals, or welfare of the citizens.'" *The New York Times,* June 1, 1950.

[2] In a speech before a meeting of the Regional Plan Association in New York City on October 10, 1950, as reported in *The New York Times* October 11, 1950.

with windows. Its publicity program promotes their sale
by shrill propaganda in the press and on the air.

The FHA, more than a decade ago, boasted of its high-
pressure salesmanship methods. For example:

"Increased volumes of small-home loans are expected
from the intensive advertising campaigns being planned
. . . by many members of the building industry, campaigns in which the FHA is prepared to lend concrete
assistance. The campaign, which has the full support of
the FHA, is being keyed especially to the interests of
families in the lower income brackets and will stress the
favorable terms on which new small homes can now be
financed.

"While almost half of the more than 450,000 families
now purchasing homes under the FHA plan have incomes
of less than $2500 a year, it is believed that the market for
homes represented by families in this income category can
be greatly expanded if the possibilities of home ownership
are adequately and continuously presented to them. . . .
The FHA, as its contribution to the national program, will
offer new display booklet, newspaper and radio advertising material, and other assistance." [1]

This sales campaign—publicity paid for by the taxpayer
—seems the more dangerous the more closely it is examined. As John P. Dean puts it in the best analysis of home
ownership to date: [2] "If a family makes a bad mistake in
purchasing food, clothing or rented shelter, a correction
is possible within a reasonable span of time. In the home

---

[1] Insured Mortgage Portfolio: *A New Small-Home Ownership Program*, February, 1940, pp. 3–4.

[2] John P. Dean: *Home Ownership, Is it Sound?* (New York: Harper
& Brothers; 1945), p. 66.

ownership field, the market is not self-correcting, and it is especially costly to learn by experience."

9

What are the arguments in favor of home ownership?

This may appear to be a foolish question. The association of home ownership with economic security and moral virtue involves feelings deeply rooted in the history of mankind. The assumption that a home owner is more praiseworthy than a tenant, that a community of home "owners" (instalment buyers) is more respectable than a community of renters, seems obvious to many people. To question it seems like challenging one of the eternal verities.

Chambers of commerce and real estate boards are joined with government in a chorus of praise of home ownership.

Some people have had the temerity to suggest that the enthusiasm of business interests for home ownership has a connection with the fact that the man who is paying for his home on the instalment plan is an especially docile worker. He fears that loss of his job, or a strike which will interrupt his weekly earnings, may mean loss of his home. Although there may be difference of opinion as to the reason, there is no denying the fact that spokesmen for big business, including many who complain of government "interference" in other fields, welcome government intervention in promoting home ownership.

What are the supposed benefits to the individual and to the community from widespread ownership by people of all income levels? Here are the principal ones:

1) *The sense of contentment and security felt by the family.*

Actually, unusual expenses for maintenance often undermine the home buyer's peace of mind. These outlays, many of which cannot be foreseen, eat up money set aside for vacations or saved for emergencies such as a new baby or a spell of illness. A man may occasionally experience a glow of enthusiasm when he rolls his tongue over the announcement, "I own my home." But behind this brave statement lurks the perpetual dread of unexpected and, therefore, unbudgeted expense.

2) *Additional self-respect from occupying a house owned by the family.*

This is illusory. The real owner of the house is the holder of the mortgage—who refrains from taking possession so long as payments are maintained. Once the head of the family loses his job, the true nature of home ownership becomes painfully clear. Few home buyers realize that the average employee remains with the average employer only about three years.

3) *Freedom to make improvements or alterations without asking the landlord's permission.*

If "the owner" realized his true position, his feelings might be just the reverse. The fact is that the unforeseen maintenance costs are apt to swallow up all, and more than all, of the money set aside for improvements.

The man who rents a home can vary the size to meet

his varying needs. The owner-occupant cannot. As a general rule, the family will consist of only two persons at first. Normally, over the years it will grow to three, four, five, or more. In later years, the trend is reversed, as the children marry and want homes of their own. Occupants of the parental roof may again dwindle to two. The man who purchases a home will be burdened, so long as he owns it, with a house that, in all probability, during much of his lifetime, will be either too large or too small for his needs.

4) *Additional prestige among friends and in business associations.* For example, the home owner is usually considered a better credit risk for loans or instalment buying.

There is no doubt about the added prestige. But it may be questioned whether the man who has a $1,000 equity in an over-priced house is a better credit risk than the neighbor who lives in a rented house—but has $1,000 in the savings bank.

5) *Clear title to a home at the end of twenty-five years instead of a batch of rent receipts.*

A low-income family is forced to select a house which is low in original cost. This confines the choice to small houses, cheaply built of poor materials. In twenty-five or thirty years, such a house is apt to be of very little residual value. Actually, few families in any community will be found in the same houses they bought from builders twenty-five years before.

So much for the "good reasons" that people give for buying houses. There is, however, one chief and compelling reason—the "real reason," as a psychologist would say —why a family obligates itself for a quarter-century of mortgage payments. In the words of C. F. Lewis of the

Buhl Foundation, Pittsburgh, ". . . so many American families have bought homes, often jerry-built homes, from speculators . . . because there was no decent alternative."

10

Purchase of a house is more than the acquisition of shelter. It is and should be regarded as a real estate investment.

Is this kind of real estate considered attractive by investors generally? Emphatically not. Office buildings, apartment houses, loft buildings, and stores are continuously bought and sold as investments. But financial institutions and wise investors steer clear of small homes.[1]

A principal reason is that purchase of a one-family house involves factors that even an expert finds it difficult to appraise. The soundness of construction and the adequacy of room and closet size can be evaluated by an experienced investor. But other important questions cannot be answered with certainty.

Will the character of the neighborhood change? Will people like this bleak little house twenty-five years from now? Unable to find the answers, the professional investor turns thumbs down on the small house. He prefers

---

[1] It is interesting to note that in Switzerland and some other countries, individual apartments in co-operative housing projects are a common form of investment. The purchaser leases the apartment on an annual basis—or for a longer period—to a tenant.

to buy the *mortgages* on such houses and let the occupants assume the risks of ownership. The average family, much less informed and much less able to risk its money, buys on faith and hope. No charity is involved.

An economic depression of serious proportions would be aggravated by widespread home ownership among low-income families. This is contrary to popular belief but demonstrably true.

The tenant who suffers a pay cut or dismissal can move into cheaper quarters or double up with relatives during hard times. To the wage earner who is buying a house on the instalment plan, loss of his job may lead to loss of his home and all of the savings he has invested in it.

"Many thousands of veterans and others are being forced to buy homes they cannot afford and will be unable to pay for. This is a repetition of the conditions which caused the unprecedented mortgage panic of the nineteen thirties with its attendant obliteration of thousands of lending institutions and the loss of billions of dollars to millions of people of small means."[1]

When millions of families with incomes of $2000 or $2500 or $3000 a year are tied to contracts that compel them to use 22 cents out of every dollar income for mortgage payments on a house, and when there is no escape from this trap for a quarter of a century—it is high time to stop and consider the possible consequences.[2]

---

[1] Statement made by John W. Fahey, commissioner of the Federal Home Loan Bank, in a message sent to the United States Savings and Loan League during a meeting of the organization in Milwaukee, Wisconsin, and quoted in *The New York Times*, November 21, 1946.

[2] Statistics from: "Purchasers' Income and New-Home Financing" and "Family Income and New Rental Housing" in the *Monthly Labor Review* for July 1951, published by the U. S. Department of Labor's Bureau of Labor Statistics.

A wave of foreclosures might become a threat to the stability of lending institutions and a psychological spur to panic. It is difficult to conceive of any more potent force to move great numbers of people to listen to the wiles of a silver-tongued would-be dictator than a depression which threatened them with loss of the beloved homes on which they had been making payments for many years and which they fondly believed they owned. When people feel themselves betrayed by democratic government, they are ripe for a demagogue who paints a rosy picture of totalitarian dictatorship.

11

The FHA is guilty of financing a publicity campaign that conceals essential facts from the unsuspecting buyer. This government agency has used the mails, the newspapers, and the radio to proclaim the advantages of buying a home while concealing the dangers. Worse still, the FHA, if it does not encourage, at least permits, the publication of advertisements that misrepresent the cost of the product to a degree that normally would invite the attention of the Federal Trade Commission.

A radical change in the policies of this government agency in regard to loans on small homes is long overdue.[1]

---

[1] FHA policies on loans for construction of *apartment house* projects are discussed in Chapter VI.

1) The Federal government which assists in financing the construction of small houses, should require that all advertisements and literature include accurate and complete estimates of overall costs. Such phrases as "$72.60 a month pays all" are misleading. They should be forbidden in the advertising of any houses financed through FHA. Instead, the real cost, including maintenance, repairs, utilities, and other items—amounting to about 50% more —should be clearly stated.

FHA literature should set forth not only the benefits, but, also, the dangers and pitfalls of home ownership. The FHA should stop trying to be a "profit producing sales tool for realtors" and should become, instead, an instrument for the protection of the home buyer. Direct loans to veterans for home buying should be stopped. It is wrong for the government to encourage any veteran to put his head in a noose.

2) The Federal government should require that the essential facts and specifications of a house with an FHA insured mortgage are disclosed in the advertising. Of all of the facts, one of the most important is the habitable floor area. This is a measure which is useful because it is real. To describe a dwelling as a "one-bedroom house" or a "four-and-a-half-room apartment" is almost meaningless. The FHA should require that advertisements of dwellings, in the financing of which it participates, should include a statement of size in square feet.[1]

---

[1] In Britain the normal three-bedroom house is required by the Ministry of Health to have a total floor area of 900 to 950 square feet. The 1949 Housing Manual prescribed a schedule of sizes ranging from 750 to 800 square feet for the two-bedroom (four-person) house up to 1100 to 1175 square feet for the four-bedroom (seven-person) house.

PERCENT OF NEW DWELLING UNITS BUILT FOR RENT

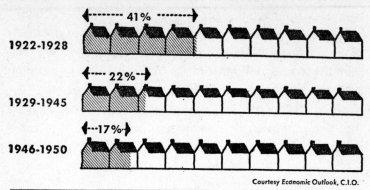

Courtesy Economic Outlook, C.I.O.

3) "About 80% of the housing now being built is for sale, although veterans and others with families of uncertain future size and jobs of uncertain tenure would much prefer to rent." [1] The government should, in fairness to middle-income families, adopt a program to promote construction of *rental* housing on a scale commensurate with the urgent demand for homes costing $40 to $65 a month, including utilities. The people who need these homes are entitled to a free choice as between renting and buying. They are denied that choice today.

Government policy should be directed toward providing—through private and public housing—a sufficient supply of new homes at such monthly costs as will offer home seekers in all income groups freedom of choice between renting and buying. If in doubt, it is safer to sign an agreement to make monthly payments for one or two years than for twenty or thirty years. If you rent, you can

---

[1] *The Economic Report of the President to the Congress* January 7, 1949 (Washington: U. S. Government Printing Office; 1949), p. 71.

change your mind and buy. If you buy, it may be too late to change your mind.

Under conditions of modern civilization, a man does not have to buy a cow because his family needs milk. He should not have to buy a house because his family needs a home.

V. *The Forgotten Third of a Nation*

1

MIDDLE-INCOME families are traditionally called the back-bone of America. Among their number are the great mass of white collar workers, a large proportion of the rural population, and the bulk of labor union membership.

But if you are a middle-income family, your housing needs are ignored. Private building enterprise is doing little for you. The Congress has consistently refused to heed your needs.

Since the close of World War II, government at all levels has launched programs, however inadequate, designed to improve housing conditions for families in the lowest-income third. The Federal Housing Administration (FHA) has spurred construction of high-priced apartments and houses for the top-income third.

If you earn $30 to $50 a week, the public housing program is for *you*. If you earn $80 a week or more, the FHA program is for *you*. But if your family income falls between those limits, you are in the middle-income group: you are one of the forgotten third of the nation.

The notion that an income of $60 to $80 a week is

enough to provide a family with good housing has been ceaselessly promoted by the literature, advertising, and publicity of real estate interests and building materials concerns.

Typical is this United Press feature article from Detroit: [1] "A nationwide campaign to show families with incomes as low as $61.54 a week how they can afford to buy 'good, substantial American homes' opened here today. Backed by the National Retail Lumber Dealers Association and the United States Savings and Loan League, leaders of the campaign figure the average family can spend 25 per cent of its income on housing. 'We went at the problem backwards,' Ted Baldwin, program co-ordinator, explained. 'Instead of people deciding what kind of home they want and then trying to stretch their incomes to cover it, we took the budget and fitted the house into it.

" 'A Detroit family—mom and pop and two youngsters —could make the $8300 house and their $60 weekly income match nicely. Mr. and Mrs. Detroiter can afford to pay out one-fourth of their $3200 yearly salaries, or $61.54 a month, for housing. On the face of it, the $8300 house seems to cost more than they can afford. But, by paying only $400 down and financing the rest over a 25-year period, the family can buy such a house for $57.18 a month —principal, interest, taxes, and insurance.' "

Note that this campaign was sponsored by two of the largest and wealthiest trade associations in the country— organizations with adequate research staffs. *The National Retail Lumber Dealers Association and the United States Savings and Loan League know very well that cost of*

---

[1] January 22, 1950.

capital, insurance, and taxes do not comprise the whole cost of shelter.

What is the true monthly cost of this $8300 house?

Interest, amortization, taxes, and insurance	$57.18
Fuel for heating	10.00
Gas and electricity	6.00
Water	2.00
Garbage disposal	1.50
Upkeep and repairs	10.00
TOTAL MONTHLY COST OF HOUSE	$86.68

By the sound old rule of thumb, a family should not pay out more each month for shelter, including utilities, than one week's net income. According to this rule, Mr. and Mrs. Detroiter should not pay more than $60 to $62 a month for their housing. *The true monthly cost of the house described in the newspaper article is more than $86. This is one-third of their net income.*

As conservative and reliable an authority as George C. Johnson, president of the Dime Savings Bank of Brooklyn, New York, has stated: "On a $9000 house the monthly carrying charges will total $73 to $83, depending on the type of mortgage and down payment. This total includes taxes and water, fire insurance, heat and hot water, interest and amortization. Income needed? At least $75 to $90 a week." Even Mr. Johnson's calculation omits any allowance for upkeep and repairs—an item which would add at least another $10 to the actual cost of housing.

It would seem fair to conclude that the National Retail Lumber Association and the United States Savings and Loan League are guilty of deliberate gross misrepresentation. The result for Mr. and Mrs. Detroiter—and their middle-income counterparts all over America—is the same old desperate choice: they can spend too much of their income for housing they cannot afford or they can continue to live doubled up with relatives or friends.

2

New housing produced in the United States—whether for rent or for sale—is beyond the means of the average middle-income family. In its assigned task of enabling private enterprise to supply housing for *middle-income* families, the FHA has failed. That failure deserves in all fairness to be considered against a background of the total record of the FHA.[1]

To await a prefabricated paradise or to expect technological advances to bring housing costs down sharply in the foreseeable future is to indulge in wishful thinking. If housing for middle-income families is to be produced on a scale commensurate with the need, there must be a joint attack on the problem by government and private enterprise.

There are three plans that give promise of reaching the objective: the Connecticut Plan, the so-called Straus Plan, and the housing co-operative.

One of the most promising ventures is that begun in the state of Connecticut, and described by former Governor Chester Bowles in Chapter XIII. Other states could

[1] See Chapters IV and VI.

profitably study its operation and endeavor to adapt it to their needs.

The program formulated in New York City in 1946 for unsubsidized self-supporting public housing became known as the Straus Plan because it was presented to then-Mayor William O'Dwyer on June 7, 1946 by a group of labor and veterans' organizations of which the author was chairman. Credit for developing the program properly belongs, also, to Charles Abrams, author of Chapter XII, and to Maxwell H. Tretter, then executive director of the New York City Housing Authority. Sponsoring organizations included the American Veterans Committee, the Catholic War Veterans, the Jewish War Veterans, the Dressmakers Joint Board of the International Ladies Garment Workers Union, and others.

The group proposed that the New York City Housing Authority erect public housing for rental to middle-income families who were ineligible for subsidized public housing by reason of too-large income.

The original proposal recommended the construction of garden apartments three and four stories high. Density was to be less than half that of the congested projects built in recent years by life insurance companies and the New York City Housing Authority. Rents were to be from $40 to $60 a month.

Local real estate taxes were to be charged annually at the rate of 3% of the cost of sites, as acquired. No additional taxes were to be levied on the new buildings.

The building capital would be supplied by the sale of bonds issued by the local housing authority and secured under a novel financial plan. This financial plan was the heart of the program. Two-thirds of the bond issue would be secured by a mortgage lien on the whole project. Interest and amortization of the bonds would be met by the rent—and 100% of the rent roll would be available for such use. The remaining third of the bond issue would be guaranteed by the city. Rents would be set at a level to cover interest and amortization of 100% of the bond issue; the bonds would, therefore, be self-liquidating.

There was no fear that tenants would fail to pay rent. Experience in subsidized public housing has shown that collection losses are negligible, amounting to less than one-half of one per cent. *Thus the city would not in all probability ever be called upon to make good its guarantee of one-third of the bond issue.*

So long as the bonds were self-liquidating, the city's guarantee, covering one-third of the bond issue, would not be chargeable against the city debt limit. To make sure that the bonds would *never* be included in the city debt, the plan provided for special taxes to support the city guarantee. For each $1 million of new housing, only $10,000 a year was to be raised in special taxes.[1]

After the taxes imposed for this purpose were collected for one year, the proceeds would lie in the city treasury. The money would remain there unless needed. There was, therefore, little likelihood that any tax would have to be collected after the first year. *Thus the total burden on the taxpayers, over the 50-year life of a housing project, would probably be only one per cent of the original cost.*

A project built by the New York City Housing Authority under this program, if financed at about 2% or 2½% inter-

---

[1] Six taxes have been authorized in New York City for this purpose. They cover tobacco, other than cigarettes; patent medicines; admission to amusements; telephone calls; occupancy (rents), and vending machines.

est with 45-year amortization, would provide apartments at these rents (including utilities): two rooms, about $40; four and one-half rooms, about $60.

The plan was calculated to provide large quantities of middle-income housing, all of it built on low-cost vacant land by private contractors paying prevailing wages.

3

There were three practical questions that had to be answered before the Straus plan could be termed sound and workable.

1. *Is it constitutional?* The opinion of leading law firms specializing in constitutional law was that the plan was sound and the special tax provision would meet all of the state's constitutional requirements.

2. *Is it financially feasible?* Several large banking syndicates said that a tax-exempt bond issue of which one-third would be guaranteed by the city and two-thirds would be serviced by rents, could then be marketed at an interest rate of about 2½%.

3. *Are suitable sites available at reasonable cost?* The sponsors of the plan offered to obtain sites in any of the city's boroughs except Manhattan at a cost low enough to limit density to between 25 and 50 families to the acre. Specific available sites, ranging from thirty acres to more than one hundred acres, were submitted to the mayor. On land costing $2 a square foot the proposed rents could be

achieved with a density of 50 families; at $1 a square foot, density could be held to 25 families.

The O'Dwyer administration neither accepted nor rejected the program as offered in June, 1946. For 18 months it simply did nothing. But civic and veteran organizations refused to let the plan die. A vigorous campaign was launched to push the city government into action.[1] The campaign reached a climax with a radio series entitled "A Home to Live In." Two weeks after the program was launched, Mayor O'Dwyer announced that the city would undertake a program of housing without cash subsidy.[2]

Actually, it was March of 1948 before a watered-down version of the plan which lost its unique financial provisions, was accepted and it was June, 1948 before the first project was undertaken.[3]

The operation of middle-income housing by a local housing authority is far from being an ideal solution. Public ownership and operation is not as desirable as ownership and operation by an individual, a corporation, or a tenant's co-operative.

It would seem better to have the housing authority acquire the sites and build the projects (functions which an experienced housing authority can perform efficiently and

---

[1] This was highlighted with almost daily articles by Charles Abrams in the *New York Post*.

[2] *Variety*, the trade paper of the entertainment industry, commented: "Just two weeks after independent station WMCA launched its series, 'A Home To Live In,' urging listeners to bombard City Hall with letters, the Mayor announced that a fund of $250 million would be earmarked for building during the next two years. He had been sitting on that fund since his election in 1945." (January 28, 1948).

[3] The New York City Housing Authority has built about 22,000 dwellings in 20 projects, all unsubsidized. Rents, including utilities, range from about $15.50 to $16.50 a room; for a 4½-room apartment the rent varies from about $65 to $78.

economically), and then turn the property over to the
tenants as a co-operative housing project. This would be
a good way for government to further understanding and
acceptance of the principles of co-operative housing. *Special legislation to enable tenants of unsubsidized public
housing to become the owners on a co-operative basis deserves study and enactment.*

4

An alleged weakness of this unsubsidized public housing
program is that the income from the housing authority
bonds would be exempt from Federal taxes, thus adding
to the amount of tax-exempt bonds outstanding. This argument lacks validity. There are outstanding today about
$20 billion in state and local debt which is exempt by law
from Federal government taxation. More than 80% of the
outstanding tax-exempt bonds are city or other local obligations; the balance represents state debt, but in common
usage all tax exempts are lumped together as "municipals."

If these bonds of the states and municipalities were all
subject to tax, the yield to the Federal government would
be no more than $200 million a year—and this at a cost to
state and local government of an equal amount. If such
bonds, tax exempt today, were taxed, it would merely
transfer funds from the local governments, which can ill
afford the loss, to the coffers of the Federal government.

The accusation that tax-exempt bonds are mainly bought

by rich men seeking to escape responsibility for the support of government is likewise not borne out by the facts. "The Treasury's own analysis of all returns for taxable estates since 1927 [1] shows that, on the average, only 12% of the wealth in millionaires' estates has been invested in municipals. The case against tax-exempt municipals as a vehicle of wholesale tax avoidance is, therefore, disproved by the Treasury's own figures.

"The most rapid growth of state and local debt came in the period from 1920 to 1930 when the outstanding amount of tax-exempt bonds increased from $7.8 billion to $18 billion, despite low income tax rates and, hence, despite the absence of any strong tax incentive for purchase of tax-exempt bonds. Since the 1920s were also a period of notable industrial expansion, it becomes somewhat difficult to make out any case for a 'diversion' of capital from common stocks or equity investment to tax exempt hiding places.

"Another theoretical argument against tax-exempts, that they discourage venture capital, can also be disproved factually. In the first place, there is the fact, reported above, that million dollar estates have had no more than 12% of their wealth on the average invested in tax-exempt municipals. The same sources show that the bulk of the wealth in such estates has been invested in common stocks. In the second place, the fact is that the period of most rapid growth of state and local debt, namely 1920 to 1930, was also a period of great expansion in enterprise capital." [2]

---

[1] Except 1943–44 and 1946–49, figures for which are unavailable.
[2] From an article, "The Case for Tax-Exempt Bonds" by Austin J. Tobin in *Fortune*, July, 1950.

In view of the urgent need for housing for the forgotten third of the nation, it would seem desirable to undertake the construction of two or three pilot projects according to the Straus plan. Thus it could best be determined whether this novel technique for providing housing for middle-income families at a negligible cost to the taxpayer is as sound in operation as it appears to be on paper. If so, other states should enact legislation to permit construction of housing under this financial plan.

5

A third technique for providing middle-income housing is through housing co-operatives. The ultimate solution of the housing problems of the forgotten third of a nation probably lies in co-operative enterprise, as it would offer middle-income families a way to solve their housing problems through their own initiative. This is in the American tradition. The pioneers who broke the plains could not—and did not—raise their barns or thresh their crops single-handed.

In many countries of Europe, conspicuously Sweden, Holland, and Denmark, co-operative housing has proved successful for many decades. It has rested there, as it must rest here, on sympathetic assistance from the national government and a nation-wide organization established for the specific purpose of promoting co-operative housing. A thriving co-operative movement can never take root here until the activities of small isolated groups, each concerned with a single project, are brought together in a national organization.

Here is an opportunity for one of the great foundations, endowed with funds to be expended for philanthropic purposes, to make a major contribution toward social progress at the cost of a relatively small cash outlay. A grant of $250,000 a year for two years, or a total of half a million dollars, would be sufficient to establish a national organization with a technically qualified staff, to advise and guide tenant co-operatives. Fees charged to groups making use of the services so available should defray part of the costs the second year—and, in all probability, all of the costs thereafter.

6

Policies of the Federal government have been avowedly aimed at promoting the sale of houses to rich and poor alike while neglecting the development of a much sounder method of home ownership—co-operative ownership. Bestowing its dubious blessing on instalment buying by individual families, irrespective of their financial status, the government has done little to encourage co-operative ventures.

Co-operative housing has suffered as well from the fast and loose use of the "co-operative" label by speculative builders to turn a fast dollar in the lush 1920s. Memories of these collapsed ventures have not been wiped out by the success of the relatively few genuine non-profit co-operatives. People hesitate to commit their savings and future income to a kind of venture which they associate with bankruptcy.

Like every other forward-looking movement, co-operative housing has come in for its share of attacks as "socialistic" or "communistic." Timid conservative local governments have at times taken this real estate lobby propaganda so seriously as to refuse to re-zone an area to make a co-operative project possible.

Too often co-operative ventures have been launched during an inflationary period when there is a housing shortage. Any building project undertaken in boom times —whether individually or co-operatively owned—will be imperiled by inflated costs. Overburdened by excessive mortgage debt, such a project is in danger from even a slight depression.

Sponsors of many co-operative projects have been seriously handicapped by ignorance. In dealing with land owners, architects, and contractors, they lack the technical knowledge and experience that private builders and local housing authorities have developed over the years. Charles Abrams has commented: "Co-operators are too often found organizing the venture in their spare time, trying to satisfy the tastes, hunches, misapprehensions, biases, and the special convictions of the more aggressive co-operators and their wives. The result is a final cost that dooms the venture in advance." [1] The organizers of one New York State project for fifty families held hundreds of meetings. At

---

[1] "Another String to the Bow" in *The Survey*, October, 1949, pp. 544–545.

one session a frightened lady reported she had seen a snake on the site. The group thereupon voted $50 to hire a herpetologist for a survey that revealed what any neighboring farmer could have told them: there was no danger of the co-operative children being decimated by non-co-operative reptiles.

To overcome these obstacles and make co-operative housing an important part of the American scene, three things are necessary.

First: there must be a source of technical guidance in organization and administration, including planning, construction, and management. In Europe technical assistance is usually provided by strong central organizations of housing co-operatives which work closely with local government and other public agencies. The *Tenants Treasury and Building Association* of Stockholm (known as the HSB) buys land for Swedish co-operatives, builds the projects, oversees the accounting, and keeps a supervisory eye on operation. In Denmark the *Workers Co-operative Housing Society* has guided the movement. Similar leadership, with government encouragement is essential in this country.

Second: long-term financing at low interest rates must be available through a source seriously interested in promoting co-operative housing. In the United States this means a Federal agency. The new agency should be the instrument for channeling private funds into sound and useful investment in homes for middle-income families. The philosophy and past policies of the FHA would seem to make its qualifications for this role open to question.

Third: there must be assistance from *local* governments in handling site selection, design, site planning, and provision of utilities. Most Swedish and Dutch cities actually acquire and plan the sites for co-operative projects.

In 1950, under the threat that a new Federal agency might be created to promote genuine middle-income co-operative housing, the Federal Housing Administration asked for the addition of Section 213 to the National Housing Act. For purposes of Federal mortgage insurance and assistance, this section defined a co-operative as any organization with *five* members who desired to build and own their own apartments.

Speculative builders promptly overcame their distaste for the "socialistic" and "communistic" features of co-operative housing, and rebaptized speculative apartment projects planned under Section 608 as "co-operatives" under Section 213. By collecting a small platoon of relatives, friends, or employees as "co-operators," the project could be built with government aid. By securing a proper sprinkling of World War II veterans as owner-tenants, the government insurance to which the builder was entitled could be raised to 95% of the cost.[1] Although some worth while projects have been planned under Section 213, they are outnumbered by the volume of spurious "non-profit" co-operatives which promise to become the source of another scandalous bonanza for builders rivaling that which surrounded the abandoned Section 608.

The president of the Long Island Real Estate Board, A. Edward MacDougall, warned on April 24, 1951 that many of the projected 213 "co-ops" will offer tenant-owners inadequate and badly planned suites. Mr. Mac-Dougall said: "Families will be living in these apartments

---

[1] These percentages were sharply reduced early in 1951, as one of the Federal Reserve System's methods of restricting credit extension.

for 10 or 15 years at the minimum, yet we find a $15,000,-000 213 project without separate dining spaces in its suites, still another with a second bedroom only 8 feet wide." He added that most disturbing are the glowing promises made to prospective tenant-owners in newspaper advertising and in brochures put out by the builders. "A lot of the present advertising is questionable. For example in a big three-column ad just last week the project was called 'nonprofit' three times. The builders doing these large jobs are not building for fun—they expect to make a profit." [1]

7

Great savings in monthly cost can be achieved through *genuine* co-operative housing. Here are the four principal economies:

1. *Nonprofit operation.* Obviously a co-operative does not charge a profit on land or operation against itself. The saving is at least $5 a month per dwelling.

2. *Maintenance.* Middle-income families will care for their grounds and perform other services that are covered in the rent of higher-priced apartments. This system has worked well in public housing; it should work better with co-operative owners. The saving is at least $6 a month.

3. *Vacancy and collection losses.* In FHA projects, 7% is added to rents to cover losses from vacancies or nonpayment of rent. In public housing these losses have averaged

---

[1] *World-Telegram & Sun*, April 25, 1951.

less than one-half of one per cent. For co-operative housing a safe allowance would be 2%: saving, $5 a month.

4. *Financing*. Loans for co-operative housing, if guaranteed by the government, should cost no more than 3%, including an allowance for administrative expense and adequate reserves. By spreading the amortization over the 50-year life of the project, monthly costs would be further reduced. The estimated saving is $10 to $12 a month.

All told, these four economies should bring down the cost of a co-operative dwelling by at least $25 a month. A middle-income family would pay $60 to $65 for a 4½-room dwelling, with utilities and everything else included.[1] Such rent would be practical for the great bulk of the families comprising the middle-income third. These families would be enabled to do what is now impossible: become owners of new, livable housing without unbalancing their budgets.

The case for co-operative housing is so eminently sound and the need for homes among middle-income families is so critical that the necessary legislation cannot long be delayed. A bill to launch such a program was introduced in the Congress and was, of course, attacked as an un-American venture that would lead down the red road to socialism.

There is no doubt, however, but that the issue is alive.

---

[1] Administrator Raymond M. Foley of the Housing and Home Finance Agency estimated, in testimony January 30, 1950, before the House Banking and Currency Committee, that an $8000, 4½-room dwelling would rent for $64.67 (including utilities) as against $90.32 for a comparable apartment built under section 608 of the National Housing Act. The saving would be $25.65 a month. The administrator was figuring conservatively. For example, he allowed 3% for vacancy and collection losses instead of the 2% suggested in this chapter.

The principle of co-operation for the common good is firmly rooted in American tradition. Co-operative housing enterprise would enable middle-income families to enjoy the satisfactions of home ownership while avoiding most of the risks.

VI. *A "Miraculous Piece of Legislation"*

1

THE ESTABLISHMENT of the Federal Housing Administration (FHA) by Act of Congress in 1934 marked the beginning of one of the noblest conceptions of creative government enterprise in the history of this country. Before that time, builders could borrow no more than about 60% of the cost of a home or a housing development from private sources. To obtain the balance of the capital needed, they were forced to obtain second mortgages and even third mortgages, often at usurious interest rates. By substituting a single government-insured, long-term, low interest mortgage amounting to from 80% to 95% of the total cost, the FHA performed a real service to builders as well as lenders.

The FHA also introduced the principle of *amortization* into new home financing—the practice of providing that, as a building aged and its value was reduced, the mortgage should concurrently be reduced in amount.

Not only did the FHA revolutionize the financing of homes and apartments, but its policies had a profound effect as well on the location, architecture, design and construction standards of new housing as well as the protection of the value by deed restrictions on adjacent property.

The FHA encouraged the dispersal of population from our congested cities to the suburbs. It introduced and made popular the two- and three-story suburban garden apartment, housing that held its tenants and maintained rent scales even in depression times. It encouraged originality and imagination in planning, such as curved roadways and dead-end streets, and thus broke the deadly tradition of endless rectangle patterns.

The FHA established minimum standards of design, materials, and workmanship as a condition for approval of loans. Into an industry that had been the prey of the jerry-builders and the loan sharks, the agency brought order and decency. The FHA made a real and lasting contribution to the betterment of American life.

It would be difficult indeed to convince a family living in a two-story garden apartment—a kind of development virtually unknown in this country before the advent of FHA—that there was anything wrong with the agency which made its construction possible. It would be equally difficult to convince others who shared in the project, builders and lending institutions, that this sound, adequately amortized project, financed by a long-term single mortgage, was not an improvement over the chaos which existed before the birth of FHA.

2

Any attempt to deal constructively with the total record
of a government agency faces a grave difficulty: American
public opinion has one standard of criticism for private
enterprise and another for the "bureaucrats" in Washington.

A striking example of this double standard at work
occurred in the depression days of the early 1930s when
many buildings just completed found themselves without
tenants. This fate befell even American landmarks like the
Empire State Building and the RCA Building in Rockefeller Center. For years, both remained largely empty and the
sight was so depressing that random rooms in vacant
floors were lighted from four to six o'clock on winter eve-
nings to relieve the gloom. So far as there was any public
comment, editorials and articles commended the "courage
and initiative of free enterprise in forging ahead in the
typical American spirit."

At the same time, several early housing projects were
completed by the Public Works Administration. Public
housing was new and untried in this country, but the PWA
had forged ahead, too, providing jobs in the construction
trades, where there had been stagnation, and providing
fine low-rental housing projects. However, several of the
buildings remained partly untenanted for a few months.
The result was a hue and cry from one end of the country

to the other, pointing to the part-empty buildings as proof of "bureaucratic bungling" and waste of government funds.

Similarly, when the world's most luxurious hotel was completed in New York City in the same period, some of its walls were found to leak. Despite its excellent design, layout, and construction, the flaw had to be remedied at considerable expense. But the matter passed without great public concern.

In contrast, when the walls of six buildings, out of several hundred constructed by the PWA under its low cost housing program, sprung small leaks, the result was a cross-country uproar. It mattered little that the leakage stemmed from an experiment in cost-cutting by building brick walls about two-thirds the customary thickness; that the experiment proved a success in most cases, and that the leakage involved only a tiny per cent of all buildings constructed. The New Deal was denounced for "extravagance," "bureaucratic incompetence," and "typical government fumbling."

This double standard is a real obstacle, not only to creative government striving to serve its people, but to anyone who attempts objectively to evaluate the operations of a government agency. One cannot minimize the failures without denying to the public the facts from which reforms must stem. But to point out shortcomings is to run the danger of supplying fuel to the propaganda mills of those who want to halt all government enterprise.

3

Despite its record of solid achievement, any evaluation of FHA must consider the fact that the agency has not fulfilled its assigned task of enabling private builders to provide homes within the means of middle-income families. The single family homes built through FHA aid under Section 203 of the Act, have been far too expensive for this income group. Faced with this criticism, the FHA encouraged lowering costs by lowering construction standards and reducing minimum space standards. A very large proportion of the single family houses financed with FHA insured mortgages are shoddy in construction and woefully inadequate in size. Moreover, FHA became a far-too-willing accomplice in a drive to induce families to buy homes whose real cost was beyond their incomes.[1]

As early as 1938, the original purposes for which the agency had been established were submerged to the point that its deputy administrator told a group of real estate men with exemplary candor: "The National Housing Act is a profit producing sales tool for realtors." [2]

The builder of a single-family house under Section 203 of the National Housing Act, assuming virtually no risk,

---

[1] See Chapter IV.

[2] C. C. McGehee: "Significance of New Title I Provisions and Regulations to Realtors," Proceedings of the Realtors' Housing Conference Discussing the National Housing Act (as Amended February 3, 1938), held March 17–19, 1938; Washington, Government Printing Office, 1938.

was usually able to boost his profit to about double the theoretical limit. FHA regulations allow the builder a 5% architect's fee. By purchasing a set of basic plans for about $200, which—with minor variations—will serve an entire development, he is able to pocket another profit which may run as high as 4% on each home.

The builder who buys raw undeveloped land for 500 houses is able to figure his land cost on the basis of its value *after* the development, and thus pocket an extra profit. By estimating his costs generously in his loan application, he is often able to make additional savings when he comes to purchase building materials.

There are other extras which shrewd speculative builders can squeeze out without technically violating any law. Since government-guaranteed FHA mortgages are considered unusually attractive by financial institutions, banks and insurance companies are willing to pay a fee to a builder for the privilege of loaning him money. The builder's commission on placement of such a loan for a small house development may amount to 2% or even 2½%. This, of course, is a fringe extra added to the theoretical profit limit.

While Section 203 of the National Housing Act offered realtors a "tool" for doubling the profit rate allowed on single home construction, the final debasement of FHA came through exploitation of Section 608 of the Act by apartment builders.

4

Under the provisions of Section 608 (now substantially re-enacted as Section 207) and in return for the generous financial terms afforded by the FHA, the profit on an apartment house project was theoretically limited. Yet, one can find in the real estate sections of the newspapers many apartment houses built under the provisions of Section 608, which are offered for sale by builders at prices which will give the purchaser an *annual return* of 20% to 30% on the purchase price.

Even though such advertisements may exaggerate the amount of income which the property will yield, the condition which they reveal is, indeed, an amazing one. When a builder, under Section 608,[1] erects apartments with funds provided by government guaranteed loans and then is able to sell the project at a price which gives the purchaser an annual income of 25%, it is clear evidence that the builder has been able to do something never anticipated when the FHA was established, and, indeed, at variance with its fundamental principles.

The FHA has become a government agency unique in American history. Established to assist developers to erect low-rent, limited-dividend housing, the agency has been

[1] The National Housing Act has been amended so that the section formerly known as 608 has become Section 207. However, since the projects discussed are generally known in real estate circles as "608 projects," that terminology has been adhered to throughout.

*converted into a mechanism for providing high-rent hous-
ing and fantastic profits for speculative builders.*

But this is not the whole story. An annual income of
25% or 30% on a builder's investment presumes that the
builder has invested some of his *own* money in the project.
This often is not the case. *Architectural Forum* [1] in sum-
ming up the operation of Section 608 says: "This miracu-
lous piece of legislation makes it possible for almost
anybody of moderate acumen to become an apartment
owner without spending a cent of his own money."

Assuming that you have a "moderate acumen" and no
inclination to spend your own money, how would you go
about becoming an apartment owner with, for instance, a
$300,000 apartment house as your goal? Under Section
608 the FHA insures 90% of the estimated necessary cost
of an apartment house, as well as 90% of the current value
of the land on which it is built. The FHA assumes this risk
in return for an insurance premium of one-half of one per
cent.

In theory, you, as the builder, are obliged to invest at
least 10% of the estimated necessary cost out of your own
pocket. The secret lies in the words "estimated necessary
cost." In many areas, estimated construction costs and land
costs can be well padded and still win approval of FHA
authorities. "FHA shows an optimism in going along with
nonexistent equities and inflated loans that would make a
conservative banker blanch." [2]

So the trick is to boost the estimate of land costs and
construction costs and obtain the approval of the FHA
for a loan in excess of the *actual* cost of the project.

---

[1] In an article, "Apartment Boom," January 1950.
[2] *Architectural Forum,* op. cit.

"Mere FHA approval of a 608 plan will jack up land value overnight. A speculator buys a piece of land, then secures FHA approval of a plan designed (more or less) for the site. The FHA stamp of approval enables him to sell the deal at five or six times what he paid for the land." [1]

By putting a $100,000 estimate on a piece of land for which he has paid $90,000, a builder can unload the entire land cost onto the government through the 90% provided through FHA. Similarly, by putting a $200,000 estimate on a construction job that can be brought in for $180,000, a builder can unload his entire construction cost on the government through the 90% provided by the FHA.

If a builder is unable to do this—and the practice is so common that it is known in the trade as "mortgaging out" —he may be forced *temporarily* to invest some of his own money.

There are other ways of circumventing the intent of the law. FHA allows a 5% architectural fee. A shrewd builder can usually whittle his architectural costs to an actual 1½% and pocket the difference.

Since government-guaranteed loans on apartment house projects are in demand as investments by financial institutions, banks and insurance companies will pay a substantial fee to the builder for the privilege of lending him money. Builders have actually been paid as much as 4% or 4½% commission for the placement of loans. On your $300,000 apartment house, you can obtain between $12,000 and $13,500 as a commission from the lending institution for the privilege of lending you the money to build your Section 608 project.

---

[1] Ibid.

⌐30% PROFIT⌐

2-STORY GARDEN-TYPE APT BLDG.
22 apts; rental $24 per room
Investment $30,000; Profit $9,400
ALSO 16 APARTMENTS:
Investment $22,000. Profit $6,000

JOHN MALAKOFF
280 Madison Ave. LE 2-3281

Attention Smart Investor!
'608' FOR SALE
CHOICE LOCATION!
$25,000 cash required.
25% RETURN!
No stock transfer
Write Box X 7584 Times

20% Net Return

(Plus $29,445 Amortization)

ATTRACTIVE GARDEN APARTMENT FOR SALE

Two-story, solid masonry. 256 three-and-four room units, 147
garages, modest rents. Excellent location—12½ acre plot.

$205,000 CASH REQUIRED

UNDERWOOD-CLARK COMPANY
(Exclusive Agents)
1150 Springfield Ave., Irvington, N. J. ESsex 3-9300

Two of these advertisements (upper left and bottom) appeared in a single issue of The New York Times *on February 25, 1951. The other (upper right) appeared in the same newspaper on September 16, 1951. They can be matched in the Sunday real estate sections of many large city newspapers.*

Thus, if you are not able to reimburse yourself completely, as a builder, for your theoretical 10%, or $30,000, investment in the apartment house by having a $270,000 project approved for a $300,000 loan, you can still stand a chance of "mortgaging out" by getting a 3½% kickback, or $10,500, on architect's fees and a 4% kickback, or $12,000, from the lending institution where you place the FHA mortgage. At worst, you end up owning an apartment which cost you nothing to build. That, however, is only the beginning.

If you wish no further burden in the operation of the apartment house, you can offer the apartment project for sale. You can advertise a "$300,000 apartment house" for sale. Your mythical $30,000 equity—which had cost you little or nothing—could be sold for at least $20,000 on the advertised claim that the profit from the operation of the project would yield the new owner between 20% and 30% per annum on his investment.

5

Rents in most FHA apartments range between $90 and $130 a month. These are high rents, beyond the means of the great majority of American families. Moreover the apartments which rent for less than $100 are very small units. Actually about half of all the apartments built under the Section 608 program were units of 3½ rooms or less.

A "3½-room apartment" consists of a living room, bedroom, kitchen, dining alcove. This is too small for a family with even one child. "FHA minimum standards are already substandard. Its minimum 150 square feet living room is 10 square feet less than the minimum living room acceptable to the New York City Housing Authority for a family of four. Its master bedroom minimum of 100 square feet compares with a master bedroom of 125 square feet in New York public housing.[1]

---

[1] *Architectural Forum,* op. cit.

A slight depression would certainly cause many families to vacate these small high-priced apartments.[1] "The whole FHA risk-bearing formula, which has flourished in a period of rising real estate values, has yet to meet the decisive test of a serious value decline. . . . If too many vacancies appear and mortgage payments cannot be made, the U. S. government may become the owner of $2.4 billion worth of apartment buildings. But nobody else involved in the deal will lose a cent. In fact, they all will have made money."[2]

6

When a government agency designed to improve building standards and prevent profiteering in the basic need for human shelter is converted into a "tool" for enabling

---

[1] An account which appeared in the *New York Herald Tribune* October 29, 1950, is most revealing in this connection:

FORECLOSURES ON 608 BUILDINGS RISING STEADILY

Lending some degree of weight to the opinions of observers who have stated that apartment construction was approaching the saturation point before the Korean crisis, at least from the marketing standpoint, are an interesting set of figures obtained from the Federal Housing Administration on the record of foreclosures or other distress acquisitions of so-called "608" new postwar rental apartment projects.

The number has increased steadily all this year [1950], having amounted on January 1 to a total of nineteen throughout the entire country that had been acquired by the FHA through foreclosure on mortgage notes; thirty-three by March 31; thirty-nine by June 30; and at least forty-seven by September 8.

See also *The New York Times*, November 19, 1950, Sec. VIII, p. 1 and *The Miami Herald*, July 21, 1950.

[2] *Architectural Forum*, op. cit.

speculators to make profits of 25% and more per annum, without assuming the slightest risk, the time has come for a searching re-examination of the law creating the agency and the policies under which it operates. Such a review of the FHA should have as its object the restoration of the original purposes for which the agency was established. The FHA was created:

1. To promote the construction of well-designed and well-built housing at monthly costs within the means of middle-income families by making mortgage funds available at the lowest possible interest rate to builders who are ready to provide such housing.

2. To limit the profits of builders who obtain FHA insured loans to a low stated return on actual cash investment, such return to be commensurate with the assumption by the government, under its guarantee of an 80% or 90% loan, of most of the risk normally assumed by a speculative builder.

If the FHA were so reorganized as to bring into conformity its original purposes and its actual practices, the agency could still render great service to the American people.

VII. *The Plight of the Cities*

1

IF WE could start from scratch in building the towns and
cities of the United States, would they be laid out as
they are? Would they be so ill-suited to meeting modern
living, industry, and traffic conditions? The answer is
obvious. Most American cities were originally built without any plan. Their haphazard growth was the product of
pioneering energy and human greed bent on exploiting to
the utmost the needs of a growing population.

City design—generally a succession of identical rectangles—was dictated by a very simple consideration: the
convenience of the real estate speculator. The 20-foot or
25-foot lot was the unit of trading. It had the merit of convenience in the market place. Unlike a bushel of wheat or
a pound of wool, however, every plot of land is different
from every other. While ten bushels of wheat can be added
together and merged, ten 20-foot lots are not susceptible of
similar simple addition. Contours, rock formations, and
the manifold variations of nature interpose to make it impossible to squeeze land into such a strait-jacket. The
failure of the attempt is dramatically evident in the aspect
of almost any city. The average American community is

unsatisfactory, whether regarded as an industrial enterprise or as an experiment in living.

If our cities were ill-suited to the life of the nineteenth
century, the effect of their shortcomings has been intensified by the life of the twentieth. The uniform rectangular
block pattern, monotonous and wasteful of space though
it was, imposed no special burden on a society that de-
pended on its feet, streetcars, and horse-drawn vehicles
for transportation.[1] The lack of zoning or any provision for
segregation of business and residential neighborhoods was
far less of a menace in a small community before the automobile had arrived. Even the failure of those who built
the cities to make adequate provision for parks and playgrounds was a less serious matter when vacant lots were
available for juvenile baseball and football and when, outside of the limits of almost every town, there were limit-
less acres for picnicking, hiking, hunting, and fishing.

The growth of the cities and the advent of the motor
vehicle have changed the pattern of city life. Hard pavements, unbroken by a tree or even a patch of lawn, have
become the environment in which millions of people must
live. Instead of a small park or oasis of green, the filling
station has become the typical disfigurement of many urban street intersections. It is a paradox that the automobile, which was to give men greater mobility, may at

---

[1] "City planners are not only able to improve property values but
often eliminate up to 40% of the streets. . . . In some of the old sections of San Francisco we feel that we can take one-half or better of the
streets out in our redevelopment program and the revised arrangement
will serve the community better, providing just as good transportation
and taking up less space." (Paul Oppermann, director of the San Francisco Planning Department and president of the American Institute of
Planners, quoted in The New York Times, March 12, 1950.) Pittsburgh
and other cities that have made progress in urban redevelopment report
similar experience.

certain hours slow traffic to a pace that would have made the horse-car driver of the 1890s curse at his slow progress.[1]

Conditions that caused only minor discomforts in the past have become serious threats to business and the business of living in the present. Factories belch their smoke and fumes in residential neighborhoods, speeding automobiles kill and maim more children than infantile paralysis, traffic jams clog our city streets.[2]

When people are huddled together in crowded buildings, the cost per family of street cleaning and waste disposal is enormously increased. That is why congested areas are usually dirty and littered. Police protection costs more, too. The taxpayer must pay for the purchase and maintenance of parks and playgrounds, recreational areas which should be, and in properly designed housing projects are, included within the development.

The evils of overcrowding in their impact on human well-being are obvious. However, the effects of overconcentration of population on urban economic life are only now coming to be understood. *Congestion on city streets constitutes a growing threat to the commercial and industrial life of our cities.*

---

[1] "Highways in the metropolitan area resembled huge parking lots yesterday as the worst traffic jams in motor travel history marred the departure of holiday vacationists. Cars were stalled in New Jersey for as long as six hours waiting to cross the Delaware River; traffic to the Catskills over Route 17 moved at five miles an hour." From *The New York Times*, July 2, 1950.

[2] The traffic toll in 1950 reached a record high, when 35,500 people were killed and 1,799,800 were maimed or injured by automobiles, trucks, taxicabs, and busses. The automobile is directly responsible for killing one child or adult on an average every three hours each day and night throughout the year. Traffic accidents cause 60% of permanent disabilities. Traffic accidents kill more children between the ages of one and fourteen than measles, scarlet fever, whooping cough, diphtheria, and infantile paralysis combined.

In the words of a qualified authority, traffic congestion and attendant evils will disintegrate large cities throughout the country as surely as an atom bomb unless remedies are applied, since "both of these powerful forces have the same effect in scattering the population, only the explosive qualities of the bomb operate more quickly. Property loss may be even greater if caused by an overwhelming traffic blight. When a city is blasted into rubble, the inhabitants, that is what is left of them, generally come back to rebuild. They seldom return to deserted communities and the billions invested in industry and construction vanish with decay. This may seem like an overstatement, but it is borne out by the migrations which already have taken place from urban areas. *The doom of New York and many other cities is written large in the overcrowded streets.*" [1]

Such conditions afflict to a greater or less extent most American cities. Until recently, they had been accepted as normal and inevitable concomitants of city life. "Literally billions of dollars of Federal funds have been poured into cities for housing which has increased concentrations of population in central city areas and encouraged formless sprawl in the suburbs." [2]

Just as many people have awakened to the fact that slum areas must be wiped out, so others have pursued a parallel line of thought to the conclusion that deficiencies in the physical aspect of the cities can and must be cured by similar surgery.

Housing and industry, buildings and highways, places

---

[1] Wilbur I. Smith, president of the Institute of Traffic Engineers, as quoted in *The New York Times*, September 29, 1949. Emphasis supplied.

[2] Paul Windels, president Regional Plan Association, Inc., of New York, in an address at the annual convention, American Institute of Architects, May 11, 1950.

to earn a livelihood and places to spend leisure should be located to fit the realities of life today. There is dawning comprehension at the beginning of the second half of the twentieth century that American cities are long overdue for replanning and rebuilding.

Much of the impetus for such thinking comes from Europe. In the Scandinavian countries, in England, Holland, and Switzerland the shortcomings of the cities as places to work and to live were recognized long ago. In the interval between the two World Wars, plans were made and carried out for rebuilding many cities. Among those in which long-range reconstruction plans have been most effective are Amsterdam, Stockholm, and Manchester.[1]

It is interesting to note that city planners abroad had one great advantage over any city planner in this country. Many municipalities owned peripheral land, originally used for fortifications to defend the inhabitants. No longer needed for its original purpose, the land was available—and in many instances utilized—for that dispersal of the population which is of the very essence of wise replanning.

2

We in this country are accustomed to think of betterment of urban living conditions in negative terms. We speak of "wiping out slums," "enforcing safety ordinances,"

---

[1] The reconstruction plan carried out in the German city of Frankfurt-am-Main during the short life of the Weimar republic, in the early 1920s, was conspicuously successful and had a profound influence elsewhere.

and "closing up firetraps." Rarely is there discussion of re-planning neighborhoods or understanding of basic princi-ples on which sound redevelopment policies must rest.

Typical of the common attitude was the praise accorded the odd little schemes that have been tried in various American cities, conspicuously Baltimore and Indianap-olis. There was nothing new about either.

The so-called "Baltimore Plan" was merely an attempt at stricter enforcement of existing building regulations. Accompanied by much newspaper publicity and beating of tom-toms, several departments of the city government undertook to compel compliance with sanitary and safety ordinances on a block by block basis. This burst of enthus-iasm for making landlords comply with regulations that had long been a dead letter, was certainly commendable. There was, however, nothing to justify the paeans of praise accorded these efforts by the conservative press of the whole country which hailed the "Baltimore Plan" as a substitute for public housing and adequate community re-development.

"Baltimore has a slum housing program. Inquiries about its operation have come from almost every state and from points as far removed as Hawaii, Brazil, and Australia. Many of these inquiries, however, represent wishful think-ing that can be traced directly to the *widespread, mislead-ing publicity given the Baltimore Plan by the National Association of Home Builders*. Through magazine articles and a $20,000 film strip, the Home Builders have repre-sented the plan as yielding 'immense dividends in health and property values,' 'gradually ridding this great metro-politan center of its slum areas,' 'providing much-needed minimum housing,' and 'markedly reducing the rate of juvenile deliquency.'

"The interest of the Home Builders in the Baltimore Plan is easy enough to explain. As part of the powerful real-estate lobby, the Home Builders are exploiting before-and-after pictures of Block Number One as evidence that slum conditions can be eliminated through private enterprise without public housing and slum-clearance programs. But anyone who believes that the Baltimore Plan is an adequate substitute for tearing down the worst slum areas and building anew is hopelessly deluded. The plan does not provide much-needed minimum housing, nor does it actually rid a city of its slum areas. . . . *The slums in Baltimore remain slums, with not a single new dwelling unit in all the jam-packed blocks.*" [1]

While the "Baltimore Plan" was useless but harmless, another similar scheme, the "Indianapolis Plan," was actually vicious. It consisted of the appropriation by the city government of Indianapolis of a sum of money to purchase and raze a portion of the large slum areas of that city without providing any homes for the unfortunate tenants. To tear down old slum buildings and evict the occupants while making no provision for housing them elsewhere is to inflict cruel hardship on low-income families. Far from improving conditions, such use of the taxpayers' money aggravates existing evils. Slum clearance should never precede the construction of new homes within the means of the families living in the area to be cleared.

---

[1] Edgar L. Jones and Burke Davis: "Slum Clearance At a Profit" in *The Atlantic Monthly*, May, 1949. Emphasis supplied.

To raze slums may be aesthetically satisfying and emotionally soothing, but it does nothing to cure the underlying cause of slums, i.e., lack of decent housing within
the means of low-income families. Stripped of the high
pressure propaganda which heralded their birth, neither
of these misbegotten offspring of real estate board lobbying and timid officialdom had anything to recommend it.

The Baltimore Plan and the Indianapolis Plan seemed
to deserve detailed description not because of either merit
or originality, in both of which they were conspicuously
lacking, but for quite the opposite reason. Each is an example of the usual techniques of the powerful real estate
lobby in deliberately deluding the people by "widespread
misleading publicity." It is safe to predict that another
scheme or plan to prove that "slum conditions can be eliminated through private enterprise without public housing"
will be launched with similar misleading publicity this
year—and as often thereafter as the real estate lobby finds
such tactics effective as a means of delaying real progress.

In the past, the limited powers and lack of funds which
confronted local communities might have offered an excuse for such inept fumbling with urban redevelopment.
"Our cities had power to plan and construct highway
systems, develop and extend their parks, and provide
schools and other municipal facilities in accordance with
population needs. But in more vital matters connected
with the growth, distribution, and development of residential, commercial, and industrial areas they were largely
powerless. At best they had only the negative controls
given them through the instruments of zoning and building codes. In that most urgent of all matters, the rebuild-

ing of decayed areas, our cities were almost wholly powerless." [1]

The Housing Act of 1949 at last has provided the tools
required to make a start at rebuilding. Under Title I, the
Urban Redevelopment section of the Act, the Federal
government can make loans to public agencies for the
acquisition of slum areas or blighted land for their clearance and preparation for rebuilding. The Act contemplates
that these lands be sold or leased for private or public
development. This must be done in accordance with plans
based on the most suitable uses of the areas and at prices
appropriate to such uses. When sold or leased at such
prices, the Federal government will stand two-thirds of
the loss. *Loans are also authorized for the acquisition of
vacant land needed for sound community growth.*

3

If we want to rebuild American cities and transform
them into better places to live and work, we might start
by listing the qualities which should characterize the rebuilt communities. Perhaps the list might read something
like this.

1. RESIDENTIAL NEIGHBORHOODS with comfortable and
attractive dwellings, located in park-like surroundings

---

[1] Speech by Warren Jay Vinton, First Assistant Commissioner, Public
Housing Administration, December 7, 1949, before the Citizen's Housing
and Planning Council of New York.

where the air is uncontaminated by smoke and industrial waste. There would be self-contained play areas designed to meet the various recreational needs of small children, youth, and adults. Many of the homes would have private gardens.

Traffic highways would be kept outside of residential groupings. Interior roads would be planned to utilize the minimum amount of space compatible with ease and convenience of circulation. The monotonous gridiron pattern of streets and avenues, which is at once wasteful of space and dangerous to life and limb, would be avoided. Ample facilities for off-street parking of automobiles would be provided, so that street parking could be strictly prohibited.

2. BUSINESS DISTRICTS, linked to the residential neighborhoods by suitable vehicular highways and so planned as to provide adequate space for parking of the cars both of workers and shoppers.

3. MANUFACTURING ZONES, separated both from business districts and residential neighborhoods by green belts, that is, parks which would serve to seperate work areas from home areas and would also provide open spaces to which people might go on week-end holidays or for more extended hours of recreation.

"The blighted residential sections of central cities should be redesigned, based on a more even distribution, a generally lower density of population and a pattern of local neighborhoods, each separated from the others by broad avenues which serve also as main traffic highways. Within these main highway borders each neighborhood should have its own interior street layout, its own schools, playgrounds, shopping centers, parking and garage facilities, public and community buildings, and other neighborhood amenities, as though each were, within the city, a separate village with its distinctive identity, interests, and community life." [1]

This blueprint of an ideal community for living and working may sound like a description of a condition which is quite unattainable. Of course, the task is one of immense difficulty. Nevertheless, the general attitude of defeatism which hangs heavy over the problem and serves to becloud all our thinking about it is quite unjustified. There is available a sufficient body of experience and also most of the basic legislation required to transform the cities and towns of the United States within a period of twenty or thirty years into such ideal communities.

To bring about the change will, however, require not only time and money but, above all, a change in the climate of public opinion. The strange timidity that afflicts most people when urban redevelopment is discussed must be overcome.

The American genius for achieving the impossible that has left its mark on so many fields of human endeavor will yet be applied to human environment. But the task cannot be undertaken, much less carried through, until the people are convinced that the goal is attainable and is worth all the time, energy, and money it may cost.

---

[1] Paul Windels, president, Regional Plan Association, Inc., of New York, in an address at the annual convention of the American Institute of Architects, Washington, D. C., May 11, 1950.

VIII. *Urban Redevelopment—Basic Principles*

1

URBAN redevelopment is an urgent need if traffic congestion is not to choke the economic life of the cities as well as blight the lives of the inhabitants. Such planned rebuilding should be preceded by (a) study of successful urban redevelopment in cities abroad and (b) preparation of a master plan of the town, city, or metropolitan area.

The chairman of the Town and Country Planning Association of Great Britain has stated the essential problem and its solution: "It is necessary to limit the growth of big cities. Redevelopment of their overcrowded areas must be coupled with a reduction of their central populations. This means expanding small towns at some distance from the metropolitan cores as well as building some new towns. This is substantially the garden city principle—creation of moderate-size industrial towns in which people live and work and do not commute."[1]

---

[1] F. J. Osborn, speaking before the Regional Plan Association, as reported in *The New York Times*, October 11, 1950.

The Housing Act of 1949 calls for "positive programs for encouraging and assisting the development of well-planned, integrated residential neighborhoods and the development or redevelopment of communities." This Act also requires the Administrator to encourage community development or redevelopment programs on a state, regional, or unified metropolitan basis. It also provides the tools for making a start.

What are the alleged insuperable obstacles in the way of realizing the dream of an America without slums, industry well located, business well served? What is it that prompts many sincere, intelligent people to believe that this hope is impossible of fulfillment?

They are:

1. *Disruption of urban life that would be involved.*
2. *The high cost.*
3. *Lack of sufficient land.*

Will a program of rebuilding require dislocation of housing and disruption of living conditions? This question looms large to people who are living with some degree of comfort today. When told of projected "green belts" and plans for "dispersion of population" they fear their own prized home will be taken over in connection with the rebuilding program. No goal however desirable seems to them worth pursuing if the price to be paid is to make life in the immediate future even more difficult than it is at present. Reactionary real estate interests have played effectively upon these fears.

When a new subway is projected or a new parkway laid out by local government, when a new real estate development is launched by private interests, there is a certain amount of disruption of neighborhood living patterns. The matter is rarely the subject of criticism on the ground of inconvenience that may be caused certain property owners. It is generally evident that the benefits will far outweigh any temporary minor drawbacks.

Planned redevelopment likewise need not unduly disturb, much less disrupt, the life of any community. On the contrary, a comprehensive project under government auspices—subject to public control and guided solely by public interest—should be even less open to justified objection.

It is undoubtedly true that the attitude of many people toward members of minority groups, especially those of different color, will add to the difficulties of an urban redevelopment program. To recognize this added difficulty, which has not confronted other countries, is not, however, to deem it insurmountable or, indeed, a reason to delay desirable replanning.

The scarecrow of "government planning" need deceive no one who does a little investigating of facts. Urban redevelopment will benefit everyone, including the merchant on Main Street and his employees who will not have to spend hours each day on commutation trains, busses and subways; the mother seeking a quiet spot to give her sleeping infant a peaceful nap, and the school child able to reach the school building without dodging automobiles and trucks. If any program for human betterment deserves universal support, it is a program which will bring the resources of technical engineering and finance—brains and money—to the task of fitting American communities to meet the needs of modern life.

2

The second objection raised to planned rebuilding is the same one always used in attempts to block progress: it will cost too much. Let it be stated at the outset that money will be needed to do the job. The $1.5 billion in loans and capital grants provided in the Housing Act of 1949 for urban redevelopment is only a beginning.

Those who would proceed slowly on urban redevelopment in fear of the cost usually favor piecemeal destruction of a slum building here, a single block there. This method of attack is more costly in the end. Whenever an attempt is made at piecemeal redevelopment, real estate in the neighborhood increases in value. Then when funds are available to take another slice out of the slum area, the cost per square foot has gone up. In the field of urban redevelopment, counsels of timidity are insurance of failure.

Those who worry about the cost of striking out boldly usually favor government action that is tentative and negative. Government must not be allowed to make an overall program for the years ahead. Positive, comprehensive planning, based on study of an ideal land use pattern for industry, business, residential purposes, is deemed dangerous, if not "communistic."

Yet, the same people who believe that the incorporated city of Philadelphia, Boston, or Little Rock should *not* indulge in planning for its future accept as normal and

proper that the duPont Company, General Motors, or the
Standard Oil Company should. They look aghast when the
people, through their duly elected representatives, try to
do for themselves exactly that which is done and is applauded in private business.

The truth is that planning is as sound for public enterprise, which we call government, as for private enterprise.
Indeed, if any human hope is to progress from dream to
reality, planning is essential.

3

Much of the cost of rebuilding American communities
could be defrayed if the community itself retained part
of the values it created by its rebuilding program. It has
been accepted practice to allow private speculators to
profit from the increase in land value resulting from the
construction of subways, highways, and bridges built with
the taxpayers' dollars. Yet, if the question is examined
dispassionately, it is difficult to see any justification for
this time-honored policy.

"When the Eighth Avenue Subway knifed its way
through vacant land areas of Queens it paved the way for
a phenomenal growth in population that added 248,678
new residents to the borough in the decade from 1940 to
1950. . . . It was the availability of unimproved land sections that proved a major factor in attracting families from
Brooklyn, Manhattan, the Bronx, and the older neighbor-

hoods of Queens. The new subway link was completed in 1933 and by 1940 there were 27.5 square miles of vacant property ready for residential construction in its wake. . . . More than 210,000 of the 248,678 new residents in Queens settled along the subway routes and in areas served by connecting bus lines. . . . Queens tripled its population from 1920 to 1950. . . ." [1]

New schools, health department branches, fire houses, and branch libraries could be paid for out of profits derived from advance purchase of land along the route of such new transit lines. Part of the land could be retained for public housing and other public uses. The balance could be sold off, when the subway or highway was nearly completed, at prices which would yield handsome profits to local government. The increment would thus benefit, not just speculative builders or speculators in land, but, instead, the people of the community. The philosophy underlying such a policy may seem unusual, but, except for the novelty, there does not seem to be any valid objection to its adoption. [2]

The appropriation of substantial sums by government will, nevertheless, be required. These expenditures of public funds will not be repaid in immediate dollar values but, instead, in permanent gains in urban living. The growing threat to industry and commerce caused by "traffic clots" will be lessened. City life will be safer and pleasanter while simultaneously it will be economically more secure.

"Some of our city officials believe the way to balance crushing municipal budgets is by piling up bigger build-

---

[1] *New York Times,* July 1, 1951.
[2] There may be constitutional questions involved that will require study.

ings which will pay higher taxes. But we can never over-
take these snowballing costs of municipal government by
intensifying the conditions which create them. If we do
not find a way gradually to bring them under control by
planned measures for orderly decentralization, we shall
witness uncontrolled decentralization, a wasteful process,
destructive of public and private values." [1]

The cost of rebuilding, like the cost of arming ourselves, will be far less than the ultimate price we will pay
for doing nothing. We *can* afford to begin—or, rather,
we cannot afford to delay.

4

The disruption of life involved in the planned rebuilding of American cities is an imaginary rather than a real
obstacle. The cost will be repaid tenfold in the benefits.
But urban redevelopment cannot be successful unless
there is enough available land. Is the strait-jacket which
confines large cities something inherent in land scarcity?

This brings us to the heart of the subject of planning.
*Fruitful discussion of urban redevelopment must begin
with the understanding of the key word—DENSITY.*
Density of population is the number of people per acre of
land.

---

[1] Paul Windels, president, Regional Plan Association, Inc., of New
York, in an address at the annual convention of the American Institute
of Architects, Washington, D. C., May 11, 1950.

If you ask a hundred people for the first inquiry they make about new housing, the answer will be almost uniform: "How much will it cost?" If you ask the same one hundred people what, in their opinion, is the second most important consideration, there will be a wide variety of answers. Few would mention the word "density." Yet the comfort and convenience of people, as well as the future economic status of a town or city will depend vitally on density of population.

In coming to grips with this key factor in planning, it should be emphasized that all low density housing is not necessarily good housing. Some of the worst slums in small towns show low population density. So-called "tourist courts" and clusters of shacks in many towns of the south and southwest are low in density but high in squalor. The buildings provide nothing but bare shelter, without any sanitary facilities or other amenities of decent living. Low density housing may be bad housing—but high density housing can never be good.

Study of population density, while it is new to us, is not new abroad.

In 1912, Sir Raymond Unwin wrote a slender volume which has become a kind of Magna Carta of city planning. It was called *Nothing Gained by Overcrowding!* and has had an influence, not only in the British Isles, but throughout most of the civilized world. The thesis of this little book was simple: housing people at a low density brings human benefits and economic gains and, since there is no scarcity of land, all new housing should be low density housing.

Sir Raymond came to this country in his later years. He lectured at Columbia University and elsewhere. He wrote for various magazines. His American speeches and articles, which embody the clearest thinking on the basic principles of planning, are not available to the general reader today. What he wrote in the 1940s is fresh and vital in the 1950s.

Sir Raymond Unwin's philosophy may be summarized as follows.

1. Urban land has no real value until a building is erected on it. So long as the land is vacant, the only value attaching to it is represented by the hope or expectation of the owner—or a prospective buyer—that it will some day have real value.

2. The validity of that hope is measured by the volume of new building. The prospect of realizing on that hope varies in inverse proportion to the densities adopted for new housing. Thus 1000 new dwellings will redeem 100 acres, if a density of 10 families to the acre be adopted; but 1000 dwellings will redeem only 10 acres if the density adopted is 100 to the acre. In this case, the owner of the 10 acres, in effect, deprives the owners of the other 90 acres of any share in the building value, the real value.

3. High density in new housing is injurious to the community by reducing the area which a given amount of new construction will redeem from blight. It is injurious to land owners by restricting the area which will acquire real value to a few acres instead of spreading the real value over a wide area. It is injurious to tenants by depriving them of space for recreation and pleasant living.

4. The density of dwellings should be determined by merit for living purposes and not by the cost of land. Desirable density should and, in the long run does, fix the real value of land.

5. The greater the density of population, the smaller will be the area which will be reclaimed by any given redevelopment program.

6. If the rehousing of slum dwellers on expensive central sites is decided upon by a local authority, the locality should be required to contribute a sum representing a proportion of the higher cost of the land. The locality will thus have a pecuniary interest in obtaining land for public housing at as reasonable a price as possible.

7. Housing on low-cost land outside the central areas of town is both desirable and practicable. This would largely solve the problems of high land cost.[1]

5

———————

Although the overall density of population in England is 17 times that of the United States, its rehousing policies for more than 30 years have been based on a density of 12 families per acre. Only a few projects in large cities show densities as high as 55 families per acre.[2]

———————

[1] Excerpts from Sir Raymond's lectures and notes are reprinted in Appendix B. The excerpts are taken from his own manuscripts given to the author.

[2] It would be desirable to discuss density in terms either of "dwellings (families) per acre," or "persons per acre." Unfortunately, such simplification is impossible. Housing statistics in general and British publications in particular, have used the term "families per acre" in the past as the measure of population density. It has come to be recognized, both abroad and in this country, that the measure is not satisfactory. Since a rehousing program provides—or should provide—for families with five and six children at one extreme and single individuals at the other, a

In the words of a great British authority on planning: "Over 90% of the inter-war houses were built on suburban estates at about twelve to the acre. The greatest advantages of this scattered development were, firstly, the light and air which each house enjoyed, and secondly, the fact that every house had a good garden.

"We made nearly four million gardens in twenty years; one-third of the fathers of Britain today spend many healthy hours each week in their gardens. I have seen thousands of these gardens, and nearly all of them are well kept. . . . To be able to do such healthy and creative work as gardening in these days of passive amusements is a boon to the men moved out from the slums. But the chief value of the garden is undoubtedly as a place for the perambulator and for the small children to play where the mother can overlook them while at work in the house, and as a place for the parents to sit in privacy and peace. The provision of these four million gardens represents an important advance in civilisation." [1]

Since 1933, long before the Labor Party came to power, local authorities in Britain have had the power to prescribe the density of all new housing—private as well as

---

more precise measurement is required. Thus "persons per acre" has come increasingly into use. While both terms are used in this discussion, an effort has been made to relate them as closely as possible.

[1] E. D. Simon: *Rebuilding Britain—A Twenty Year Plan* (London: Victor Gollancz Ltd.; 1945), p. 72.

On page 253 of the same volume, the author explains that, according to the *Report on Housing and Rehousing* of the Director of Housing of the City of Liverpool, dated December 1943, the standard of density was:

The gross density per acre of developed land varied from 9 dwellings (families) to 24 dwellings (families) per acre. The net density per acre of housing land varied from 16 dwellings to 54 dwellings per acre.

public. "It has become generally agreed that the governing principle should be density of population." [1]

In Switzerland, Holland, Sweden, Denmark—all, like Britain, densely populated countries—replanning and rebuilding have been carried out in many cities. Basic policy has invariably been to distribute the population and reduce its density.

Is there any shortage of land in the United States which would justify our rejecting these policies, accepted elsewhere and proved by long experience? Of course not. *At a density of 12 families to the acre, there is room enough for the entire population of the world in the state of Kansas. At 50 families to the acre, the entire population of the U. S. A. could be housed in the area of the smallest state, Rhode Island.*

---

[1] From an article, "World After War—No. 1: London" in the *Real Estate Reporter and Building News*, July–August 1945, New York, by Eric L. Bird, F.R.I.B.A.

IX. *Urban Redevelopment—U. S. A.*

1

WHILE some American city planners have sought to learn from Europe and profit from their solid achievements, there is another school of thought dominated by childish intellectual isolationism. This strange philosophy is exemplified by the New York City rehousing program. The guiding spirit has been City Construction Co-ordinator, Robert Moses, whose theories have established policies and whose actions have put them into effect. The New York City program is important not only because it has been very extensive, but because what the largest city in the country does is watched and emulated by other communities.

Robert Moses has rendered great service to his state and his city. The parks and parkways of the metropolitan area are largely the product of his imagination, energy, and great administrative ability. Few men in the history of New York have served the city so well. Against his great contributions, however, must be balanced gross errors in urban redevelopment. Specifically:

1. He has not only failed to produce a general overall

plan of redevelopment, but he has used his immense influence in the city government to *block* completion of one.

2. He has utilized the best residential sites, having the advantage both of bordering the East River and of being close to the heart of the business and financial districts, for public and quasi-public housing, largely tax exempt.

3. He has added to overcrowding where it already existed and created overcrowding where there was none. The evils of congestion are intensified by failure to make adequate provision for off-street parking of motor vehicles. The full impact of this disastrous policy is yet to be felt.

Mr. Moses has stated his basic principle of urban redevelopment in one significant sentence: "People just have got to move out of the way to make way for buildings that will house more families than the area has been housing." [1]

If rebuilding based on that policy is right, then Sir Raymond Unwin, Sir Patrick Abercrombie, Gordon Stephenson, Henry Wright, Lewis Mumford, and the architects who have labored to create the charm and livability of cities like Stockholm, Zurich, and Amsterdam are all wrong. The chief justification for the expense and inconvenience of moving people "out of the way" is not to increase overcrowding but to *reduce* it. A redevelopment program which proclaims as its avowed goal to crowd more families into slum areas than lived there before is doomed to failure.

It is, however, at the risk of villification that anyone ventures to question the wisdom of current redevelopment policies. At the least he is dubbed by Mr. Moses a "star gazer" or a "slap-happy smart aleck planner." If the critic is so bold as to contrast conditions of dirt, congestion, and

---

[1] As quoted in the *New York World-Telegram*, September 25, 1946.

noise on the New York City streets with cities of Europe where, as a result of wise urban redevelopment, overcrowding and slums have given away to peace, order and beauty—he is in danger of being dubbed a "beiunski." [1]

The overcrowded tenements built in eastern cities in the second half of the nineteenth century to exploit the desperate need for shelter of the immigrant tides from Europe, have become the slums that plague us today. The same overcrowding, the same disregard of the relation of housing to other aspects of city life that placed a blight on the cities in the 1880s and 1890s characterize the New York City current program. Instead of avoiding the mistakes of the last century, New York—and some other communities—are repeating them.

The sidewalks of New York, famed in song and story, are today probably the dirtiest of any large city in the world. Lofty skyscrapers as well as "old-law" tenements rise from chipped, broken, patched pavements littered with waste. Rubbish covers the backyards of huge areas of slums. The air is fouled with smoke and soot. As the city grows more crowded, these ugly concomitants of congestion grow apace.

---

[1] "Bei uns" is German for "with us" and is used by immigrants from German speaking countries in referring to the countries of their origin. Apparently, to Mr. Moses, any doubt as to his infallibility smacks of lack of patriotism.

2

Amazing as it may seem, there is no master plan of New York City.[1] Sober-minded individuals have called attention to the price we pay for lack of planning in ever increasing traffic congestion, dirty sidewalks, streets clogged by permanently parked automobiles under which garbage lies for days and weeks. Less evident to eye and nose— but almost as serious—the finest residential sites along the East River are being removed from the tax rolls and utilized for tax-exempt public housing.[2]

Planning is generally accepted as an essential prerequisite to action in any field. We take it for granted that the man who starts to create something has a fairly clear idea of what he wants it to look like when he has finished. Only in the field of rebuilding a city is it deemed by some people unnecessary to begin by making a plan.

The highways that crisscross the country were not built

---

[1] According to a report by Jerry Finkelstein, former chairman of the City Planning Commission (February 1, 1950), "barely 25 per cent of the work on the Master Plan [of New York City] has been advanced." New York City is by no means unique in this respect.

[2] "Practically the entire East River waterfront from 14th Street to Brooklyn Bridge is taken up with public housing for lower income groups . . . The choicer waterfront locations which might be developed by private enterprise are thus preempted. It is, of course, less probable that private builders will develop interior locations on the lower East Side than those on the waterfront." Herman T. Stichman, New York State Housing Commissioner, as quoted in the New York *World-Telegram and Sun*, May 2, 1951.

as the result of whims of various automobile owners. They were the product of careful planning by qualified experts intent upon building for the benefit of the traveling public. The network of airports, which have been a major factor in lifting American aviation to its position of leadership, were built, not by private speculators solely for private gain, but were the product of government planning. If human experience is any guide, similar philosophy and similar action applied to the field of urban redevelopment would produce similar results.

3

The best analysis of the New York City housing program of the last decade has been written by Lewis Mumford, whose studies of the problems of urbanism in Europe and the United States have earned him international recognition.

Mr. Mumford writes as follows.[1]

"For the last dozen years, the New York City Housing Authority has been carrying out a vast program of slum clearance and rehousing. It has done more in that time to improve the living quarters of the lowest-income groups than all the earlier housing reformers did in a hundred. Acres of dark, musty, verminous, overcrowded tenements

[1] These quotations, from articles which appeared in *The New Yorker* on May 6 and 20, 1950 and February 3, 1951, are reprinted by permission of the magazine and the author.

have been replaced by clean, well-lighted, sanitary quarters—also overcrowded. . . .

"It will take forty to sixty years to amortize these congested buildings, and they are constructed soundly enough to last at least a century, so while the good they do is temporary, the damage they do to the city may be permanent. . . .

"These new buildings are plainly superior in every respect to the dark, congested, insanitary, rat-infested Manhattan slums they have replaced . . . But this comparison is tricky. . . . The most disturbing thing about these new quarters is that—except in a few minor examples on the outskirts of the city . . . the land is as densely populated as it was when it was covered with overcrowded slums. Worse than that, in Brooklyn and Queens, on land once occupied by two- and three-story frame houses with generous private back yards, the same pattern of density has been introduced. . . .

"These buildings continue the old New York habit of bringing too many people together in one place at one time—in a part of the city where every new office worker or customer adds just so much more to the overburden the city's streets and transportation systems are handling and pushes the metropolis just so much closer to the point at which it will be impossible to do the very business this overcrowding is supposed to promote. . . . These oversized buildings are conceived in an obsolete pattern in a dangerously obsolete city. . . .

"The Johnson Houses supply quarters to 5088 people on 11.9 acres of land, or a density of 427 people an acre. The Jacob Riis Houses hold 6728 people on 17.6 acres, or 382 an acre, and the Lillian Wald Houses contain 7168 people on 16.5 acres, or 434 people an acre. The most densely populated of our housing estates, the John L. Elliott Houses, on Chelsea Park, packs in 497 to an acre, and the lowest density, except on the edges of the city, is 209 per acre. In general, the projects house from 300 to 450 per acre. . . .

"The open spaces, overpaved and underplanted, are downright bleak. They lack both a sufficient supply of benches and a sufficient supply of interesting objects near at hand to entertain the eye, and the heat that rises from the paved areas in summer adds to the normal discomforts of hot weather on the lower floors, thus pointing up most emphatically the inadequacy of the interior ventilation. . . .

"Against the physical improvements in the flats provided by the new housing, one must set the massive damage high-density housing has done, and threatens to do, to the city. If New York continues to be made over in this fashion, the ensuing congestion will throttle it . . .

"Temporary and futile palliatives of the kind so avidly proposed by Mr. Robert Moses (more super-highways and tunnels to pump more people into the suffocating center of the city) will absorb funds badly needed for schools, hospitals, homes for the aged, libraries, and other facilities already in stringently short supply. . . . The city could, even at present land values, save a great deal of money by building one-story schools of a new and flexible design. But the school authorities, while admitting the desirability and the probable economy of such buildings, plaintively replied that 'the erection of these great building-canyon areas, to densities of four hundred to six hundred people to the acre,' in the new housing proj-

ects would force them to 'fill the Hudson River' to get the
requisite space. . . .

"Such economies as the Housing Authority has effected
by its intensified occupancy of the land are only first-cost
economies. The final effect upon the municipal budget is
disasterous. . . . The fourteen thousand people who live
on the thirty-four acres occupied by the adjoining Jacob
Riis and Lillian Wald Houses, in lower East Side Manhattan, haven't a single church or synagogue or motion-
picture house or public market within their whole area.
The provision of these facilities, in low, freestanding
buildings, would do more to compensate for the bleak
uniformity of the huge brick prisms the tenants occupy
than any amount of fancy ornament. There is no architectural substitute for the variety and stir and color of a real
neighborhood. . . .

"It is opaque bureaucratic formalism to go on with
urban housing developments whose density of population
averages over three hundred and fifty to the acre, ignor-
ing the effect of such congestion on the transportation
systems, the street traffic, the park and playground space,
and the neighborhood schools. The core of this concept
of housing is not a family, a neighborhood, and a livable
city but an elevator shaft. . . .

"As for the Housing Authority, it is time that it retraced
its steps to Harlem River Houses (in upper Manhattan)
and Williamsburg Houses (in Brooklyn) both built a
dozen years ago.[1]

---

[1] Both projects were built when Fiorello La Guardia was mayor and
Gerard Swope was the chairman of the New York City Housing Authority
—in close co-operation with the United States Housing Authority of
which the author was then Administrator.

"Should we go on rebuilding New York on the obsolete patterns of Parkchester, Stuyvesant Town, and the municipal housing projects, we should merely be exchanging slums for super-slums. . . . If this new pattern of building becomes more widely imitated, it will create urban disabilities that will be more difficult to remove than the old slums."

4

Defenders of this policy of congestion and confusion rest their case on three assumptions. All of them are false.

1. *The fallacy:* there is not enough land to house the total population at a density that would provide good living conditions.

The fact: in the late 1930s, when the New York City post-war building program was launched, more than 30% of the area of the city, or more than 58,000 acres, was vacant or occupied by unused streets. If one-third of this vacant area had been utilized for residential purposes—about the normal proportion—nearly two million more people could have been accommodated at a density of no more than 100 persons to the acre. Yet the Housing Authority has planned its projects at an average density of more than 350 to the acre. Even in 1951, about 20% of the area of the Greater City is vacant land.

2. *The fallacy:* it is unfair to compare the density of housing projects, characterized by tall buildings from

twelve to seventeen stories high, with British and Scandinavian housing, which is only from one to five stories high.

The fact: while undoubtly the evils of overcrowding are lessened when the overcrowding is vertical so that large open spaces are left vacant between the buildings, the claim that high-density housing may be good housing if the buildings are high enough is a dangerous half-truth.

No matter how high the structures may rise or no matter how small a proportion of a given site is built upon, the effects of overcrowding are inescapable. The playgrounds will be just as congested and unplayable; residents seeking a little peace in the landscaped area at the close of the day will be just as jostled by their neighbors whether they are housed in two-story or twenty-story buildings. During the morning hour of departure for work and again during the afternoon hour of return, the roads leading to and from the project area will be just as choked with cars and busses. *At 400 people to the acre, four people must share the open space that one person would enjoy at the rate of 100 to the acre.*

3. *The fallacy:* New Yorkers—and other people who live in the big cities—prefer to be crowded into high buildings in close proximity with their neighbors.

The fact: obviously, if the only alternative to a cold-water flat, with airless rooms and dirty hallways, is a new, clean home in a building with modern bathrooms, a family from the slums will welcome an opportunity of moving into the new building even if it is fifty stories high and covers 90% of the building site. To cite this as evidence that slum families—or, indeed, American families of higher income—prefer congestion and overcrowding is sheer nonsense. New Yorkers, Chicagoans, and other Americans, just as people the world over, prefer privacy and even a little patch of garden of their own. Every poll of housing preference has shown this.

Moreover, the evidence in the growth of suburban communities surrounding all of the cities is more convincing than any poll. Millions are so eager to escape from noisy congestion that they accept the grim alternative of commuting daily to the suburbs in crowded trains and even more crowded subways. *People live in cramped skyscraper apartments not by choice, but by lack of choice.*

"Nothing is more stupid than the vicious circle we find in our larger cities, where land is worth more because you can put more people on it, therefore you put more people on it, so therefore it becomes worth more." [1]

5

The objection to high buildings, whether in housing developments or in commercial and business districts, is not to the height as such. The American skyscraper, especially in commercial districts, has proved its many advantages. Anyone who has spent a day in the business district of New York, Pittsburgh, Houston or Chicago, where transportation is largely vertical and then spent the next day in Washington, D. C., where miles of corridors in govern-

---

[1] Ralph T. Walker, president of the American Institute of Architects, in a speech before a meeting of the A.I.A., May 12, 1950.

ment buildings must be traversed horizontally on foot, will agree that the skyscraper saves time, temper, and fatigue. The real objection to the skyscraper is inherent, not in its height, but in the number of people which too many tall buildings crowd together into a small area.

Pointing out the proper function of the skyscraper in a modern city, the famous French architect, Le Corbusier, has this to say: "In place of so many small, scattered skyscrapers, a few large ones will be set up in groups. Distance will be overcome. And hours will be saved and usable. . . . No longer will it be necessary for people to jostle each other on foot or in chained vehicles in a labyrinth of streets during rush hours. *Business communities will be vertical, set in the midst of immense green parks.*" [1]

6

Overcrowding is the real evil. Whether vertical or horizontal, it should be prevented in both residential and business districts.

In residential areas, a limitation based on the number of persons housed per acre is an effective method of preventing overcrowding. However, another kind of measurement must be devised for industrial and business areas. In those parts of any city devoted to commerce, the population at night, the number of people who live in the area, is not the matter of paramount importance. The much

---

[1] Le Corbusier: *When the Cathedrals Were White* (New York: Reynal & Hitchcock; 1947), p. 68. Emphasis supplied.

larger population during the daytime hours must be limited if overcrowding, evidenced by traffic congestion on the adjoining streets, is to be avoided. *A type of regulation should be sought which would limit not only the bulk of the building but the number of people who use it during working hours. Fortunately, there is a simple way of doing this—by limiting the floor area.*

This is how it would work. The Equitable Building (40 stories) at 120 Broadway, New York City, is generally acknowledged to be one of the most extreme specimens of overcrowding in the world. In fact, the consternation of owners and tenants of neighboring buildings when this monster arose in 1915 to shut off their light and air is generally credited with giving impetus to the enactment of the first city zoning ordinances. The total floor space in the Equitable Building is approximately 28 times the area of the building site.

The floor space of the Empire State Building (102 stories), built in 1931, is 25 times the area of the building site.[1] Most of the office buildings erected in the large cities of the country since World War II have floor space at least 20 times as great as the area of the site. However, the floor space of Rockefeller Center, erected in 1931 and 1932, is only 12 times the site area and Lever House (22 stories) on Park Avenue, New York City, perhaps the finest post-war office building in the country, has total floor space equal to only 6 times the site area.

Floor space roughly determines the number of people who will spend their working hours in any office building.

[1] The inadequacy of regulations requiring set-backs and limiting ground coverage to meet the real problem is strikingly evidenced by the fact that, in spite of many regulations, the essential evil of these large buildings—overcongestion—had not been touched.

Thus it becomes a good measure of density of population during working hours. Unlike the complex language and technical details involved in most methods of limiting the bulk of buildings, a limitation of total floor area could be couched in the simplest terms. All that would be necessary would be to require that the buildings in a given zone should not exceed in total floor area a given multiple of the building site.[1] *As a basis for discussion, it might be well to consider limiting floor area of office buildings to 10 times the area of the site.* Different standards might be set for different parts of a city.

The real evil of the skyscraper, which is not inherent in its height, will be avoided and its many advantages will be retained, when adequate limitations of floor area are imposed by law.

The enactment of such a regulation would limit population density in commercial and business zones paralleling the limitation of permissible number of family units per acre in residential neighborhoods. Together these two simple regulations would constitute a sound basis for an urban redevelopment program in any city.

7

There is today on the statute books Federal legislation which makes available to any community legal power and financial grants sufficient to begin replanning and rebuild-

---

[1] The limitation of *ground* coverage to a certain percentage of the building site, which is embodied in most city building codes, should, of course, be retained.

ing on a scale never possible in the past. Effective use of these powers may require further legislation. Even more essential is a change in administrative policies—of Federal, state, and local governments—based on a grasp of overall planning and of the importance of density.

These steps will pave the way.

1. The Housing and Home Finance Agency should adopt a declaration of policy, embodying the principle that Federal aid will be granted for redevelopment schemes only provided they conform to certain standards.

Definitions of terms are essential. A "6-room house" or a "4½-room apartment" may mean a dwelling of 400 square feet or 1000 square feet. A housing project described as having "an acre of parks for use of tenants" or having "buildings which cover only 25% of the site" may be livable and uncrowded or may be, instead, a new superslum with fancy gadgets, colored tile baths—and 500 people packed into every acre. The only dependable measures of congestion are (a) size of the dwelling and (b) the number of persons living on an acre of ground.

In residential areas good housing means dwellings with an area of at least 750 to 800 square feet located in a neighborhood or housing development with a density of not more than about 100 person (30 families) per acre and with at least 10 acres of open space per 1000 persons. In business zones, acceptable density is achieved when the floor area of the building is not more than about 10 times the area of the site.

Irrespective of the exact figures chosen, the very fact that such limitations were set forth in a government declaration of policy would mark a big step forward in wise replanning.

2. Cities and towns should establish planning commissions clothed with adequate power to proceed under Title I of the Housing Act of 1949.

It is an amazing fact that most of the cities of the country have not set minimum standards of acceptability of a "dwelling," much less made a census of the number of occupied dwellings that fail to conform to the standard. A survey of present conditions and a "regional plan" to guide future development must be the starting point for sound replanning. The survey should cover such matters as identification of the slum areas of the city, the number of dwelling units which should be replaced, delineation of areas of blight or incipient blight, unsuitable land use, and faulty zoning.

3. When man-made political boundaries stand in the way of redevelopment for maximum economic efficiency and human well-being, it seems obvious that the boundaries, whatever their original purpose, have outlived their usefulness. In many of the large cities redevelopment will require the use of land not included within the municipal boundaries.[1]

---

[1] One of the difficulties in the expansion of the boundaries of any city is the fact that tax rates in the suburbs, outside the city limits, are generally lower than in the city. Thus home owners, landlords, and real estate interests in the suburbs are united in opposition to enlarging the boundaries of the city so as to include *their* property within its limits.

In Boston, for instance, planning to redevelop the "Boston area" as a whole has been defeated by this attitude of neighboring suburban communities. The taxpayers of those communities are confused as to the benefits of replanning and rebuilding, but they are well aware of the immediate cost to them of the tax increase if their real estate were taxed at the same rate as property within the Boston city limits. Thus, the

There are three possible methods of overcoming this obstacle.

i. The creation of city-states with the same sovereign powers as the present forty-eight states of the union out of the larger metropolitan areas of the country. (This suggestion was originally made by Charles R. Merriam, Chicago political scientist.)

ii. The enactment of legislation to allow cities to grow by the simple expedient of annexation of the suburbs. (This is permitted under the laws of one state, Virginia.)

iii. The establishment by state legislative action of regional or interstate authorities on the pattern of the TVA or the Port of New York Authority or the St. Louis Bi-State Development Agency. The authority, acting under state law, would have power to formulate a plan, to buy and resell land, as well as to promulgate zoning regulations and land use limitations in connection with carrying out the plan.

A method of overcoming the artificial barriers imposed by obsolete municipal boundaries is not a matter which can be disregarded. A solution is essential if urban redevelopment is to rid itself of the bonds of "city limits" and is to be free to meet real needs and achieve the real benefits of dispersion of population and industry.

4. The Federal government, in co-operation with local governments, should encourage study of site planning, town planning, and traffic problems. Courses should be established in colleges and secondary schools so that the

---

Boston Housing Authority, in planning its public housing projects, is confined within an artificial and meaningless barrier, the municipal boundary of the city of Boston.

best European and American experience in community planning and land utilization would be available to builders and town planners. Americans are not well informed on fundamental principles of urban redevelopment.

"No nation in the world spends as much of its national income on research as the United States. The great problems of military defense, of conservation of our national resources, improvement of our agriculture, development of our transportation systems, our industrial processes, and our business methods are the subject of continuous research and planning by both official and private agencies. Large annual appropriations are made by national foundations for the advancement of the physical, medical, and social sciences.

"It is a startling fact, however, that the creation of comfortable and efficient forms of city and town life, of supreme importance to our future, is today barely touched by research.

"There should be established a National Commission on Urban Population Distribution to study, report, and make recommendations on trends in population movement to and within urban areas." [1]

American communities might provide an environment conducive to economic stability and human happiness far beyond what most people believe possible today. However, there are few types of political action that require such understanding on the part of the voters as redevelopment of a community, involving their workshops and offices, their homes and their very lives.

---

[1] Paul Windels, op. cit.

There is no shortage of land or of money. There is only a shortage of understanding. Urban redevelopment will begin when the people themselves determine that they want the job done. American communities will be transformed by those who have, in the words of Justice Louis D. Brandeis, "a fire in the belly."

X. *British Housing Policies*

BY

Eric L. Bird, A.R.I.B.A.

EDITOR, THE JOURNAL OF THE
ROYAL INSTITUTE OF BRITISH ARCHITECTS

[A chapter on British housing is included in this book because the British Housing Act of 1919 created the pattern which, with minor variations, was embodied in the first permanent housing program of our own country, the United States Housing Act of 1937. These same principles were rewritten into the Housing Act of 1949.

[A second reason for inviting a distinguished Briton to report on housing is that Britain's public housing program has been misrepresented in this country as a new and revolutionary product of the Attlee Labor government. When Mr. Bird was invited to contribute this chapter, it was suggested that he include quotations from speeches of leaders of the Conservative Party to refute these charges. Mr. Bird's reply was: "I find it very difficult to produce evidence that Conservative governments support local authority housing by giving quotations from speeches because it is such an obvious and accepted fact over here. I might as well ask you to give me quotations from the speeches of American presidents that they supported the 'American Constitution! Housing is part of the accepted order of national life."

[As to his own political beliefs, Mr. Bird states: "If anyone in America reading my chapter says to you that it must have been written by a Socialist you can tell him he is wrong. If I have any politics, they are Liberal."]

1

GREAT BRITAIN has been building subsidized public housing for low-income families for thirty years. That is about twice as long as American experience in the field. By 1950, more than 1.75 million permanent dwellings in Britain had been built by local housing authorities. Thus, one dwelling out of every seven in the United Kingdom today is publicly built and owned compared with a ratio of about one out of 200 in the United States.

Public housing in Britain is regarded as a normal government-sponsored activity and has been so regarded for more than a generation. Every person is considered to have a right to a decent home and if he cannot provide it himself it is provided for him. The cost of this has long been accepted as a public expense, just as the cost of maintaining the army, the navy, or the postal system. *All schools of political thought and all political parties look upon public housing as an essential public service. All support the system of government subsidies which has been in use since 1919 in practically unchanged form.*[1]

In 1945, when a Labor government achieved full power in Parliament for the first time, this basic principle had long been accepted. Public housing, under successive Conservative and Liberal governments, had radically changed the complexion of the cities in Britain. One in ten of all dwellings in Great Britain had already been provided by local housing authorities. Some figures for typical cities are as follows. In Leeds 15% of the population, in Manchester 18%, and in Liverpool 23% were living in dwellings built by local housing authorities, before the advent of the Attlee Labor government.

[1 A typical example of misrepresentation of British housing policy is the following, quoted from a statement by a respected business leader: "Repeatedly, our Association has advocated for public housing projects a system of subsidy payments, from whatever source, that obviates the abuses that have practically everywhere arisen in connection with public housing as it has been administered in this country up to now. It is known in Great Britain as the rent rebate system, and it was used successfully there on an ever-widening scale before World War II, and before the advent of all-out socialism." (From *Housing Dictatorship and Soft Socialism*, a pamphlet published by the Urban Redevelopment Committee of the Commerce and Industry Association of New York over the signature of the chairman, Thomas S. Holden, president of the F. W. Dodge Corporation.)

[The truth is that the "rent rebate system," a kind of dole to slum landlords, was used in fewer than 200 of the more than 2000 localities in England, Wales, and Scotland which built public housing projects. The system was originally inaugurated in Leeds in 1934, but, after a trial of less than two years and a heated political campaign hinging on the issue, it was abandoned.   N. S.]

2

As in the United States, the public housing program is operated by local housing authorities.[1] However, the name "housing authority" has quite different meanings in Britain and the United States. In Britain the municipality is itself the "housing authority." Final responsibility for all action on housing matters rests with the municipal council. The council delegates most of the work to its *housing committee* which it appoints and to a permanent salaried staff which it employs.

The membership of the housing committee consists of (a) members of the council and (b) outside persons appointed by the committee. Such outside persons are chosen on the basis of their experience or interest in public housing.

The permanent salaried staff is responsible for the technical aspects of housing. It is employed by the city council and works under the housing committee. Its personnel does not change with fluctuations of party control in the council. In this it somewhat resembles the civil service.

This technical staff handles all such matters as investigations into housing needs, purchase of sites, road and sewer construction, house building, rent collection, man-

---

[1] The country is covered with a network of 1470 local housing authorities of which 81 are large city authorities, 218 medium town, 665 small town, 30 subdivisions of London, and 476 rural.

agement and repairs. The senior officials—architect, engineer, housing manager, etc.—attend the meetings of the housing committee both to advise and to receive instructions.

All expenditures for housing must be approved in lump sums by the municipal council. All contracts have to be publicly advertised and are let by the municipal council.

The dual system, consisting of a housing committee of elected unpaid members and a technical staff of paid permanent officials, works very well. The former set the problems in the light of public need. The latter supply the answers. Together, both make a final determination of policy to be followed and have it carried out. Thus there has been built up an authoritative housing technique based on long experience.

The housing committees have also educated the ordinary man and woman so that, behind British housing, there is a strong body of public opinion. Without the support of public opinion, housing would have remained a sporadic charity instead of growing into an efficient, well-understood enterprise.

Public housing schemes [1] are designed either by the municipality's own salaried architect (where there is one) or by private architects. They are financed by government loans through the Ministry of Health.[2] Since January 1951 the housing powers of the Ministry of Health have been transferred to the Ministry of Local Government and Planning.

A municipality seeking a loan submits plans and esti-

---

[1] During the planning and construction state, the project is called a "scheme." Upon occupancy it is called an "estate."

[2] The 1950 interest rate on housing loans was 3% and the loan period 60 years as against 40 years before World War II.

mates to the Ministry of Local Government and Planning, which then sends an inspector to hold a public hearing in the town. On the basis of the inspector's confidential report, the Minister decides whether or not to approve the loan. The whole system is balanced in a typically British way so that neither the Minister nor the local housing committee nor its officials can get away with dictatorial methods.

The Ministry of Local Government and Planning grants a cash subsidy to the local authority for every dwelling. This subsidy bridges the gap between the total annual expenditure of a housing authority and the money which it receives from rents. Housing authorities operate rent pools into which all money from rents goes. Rents of houses are not necessarily related exactly to the cost of individual houses when built; for instance, the tenant of a house built in 1935 for £400 may *today* be paying much the same rent as the tenant of a house built in 1950 for £1200.[1]

Despite the considerable power of municipal government, the Ministry of Local Government and Planning retains supervisory control through its control of the public purse. The Ministry also acts as a clearing house for ideas on design, planning, and building techniques. It publishes housing manuals with plans and photographs of good projects and also sets standards as to room sizes, space between buildings, and types of construction. To encourage good

---

[1] The present subsidy for a 3-bedroom (5-person) house of 900 square feet total floor area is £16.10s or $46.20 annually for 60 years. In addition, the municipal government contributes £5.10s or $15.40 a year out of taxes, making a total subsidy of $61.60 annually, or $5.13 a month. (The English pound sterling is translated here into American dollars on the basis of $2.80 per pound, the official rate. It should be realized, however, that in general the English pound buys more in Great Britain than its equivalent in dollars does in the United States.)

design and layout, the Ministry awards medals to projects of outstanding merit chosen by juries of experts.

3

Public housing in Britain was started in a small way as far back as 1885, and 11,000 houses had been built by municipalities before the First World War. However, the present system virtually came into being with the Addison Act of 1919. This Act, passed through Parliament by a Liberal-Conservative coalition, introduced the principle of a government subsidy to the municipalities for working class housing. The Addison Act also set a density limit of 12 dwellings to the acre for all housing, whether public or private.

The purpose of setting the upper limit of density of housing at such a low level was to prevent overcrowding of land and, its inevitable result, the development of new slums. Incidentally, the low density limit made it possible for every family to have a small private garden—which is something that nearly every British family wants.

After the fall of Lloyd George's coalition government in 1922, Conservative or Conservative-dominated governments held power almost uninterruptedly until the Second World War.[1] *During all of these years the fundamental*

---

[1] For two short periods, there were Labor governments, but in each government Labor did not have a sufficient number of members to exercise real power without the agreement of the Conservative and Liberal Party members. Bills which did not have the support of one or both of the other party organizations could not be enacted into law.

principle of the Addison Act, the payment by the govern-
ment of subsidies to municipalities to provide low-rent
public housing, was never abandoned. Underlining the
non-political character of public housing is the fact that,
up to the beginning of World War II, the two peak years
in public housing construction were under Conservative
governments. Those were 1928 and 1939.

By the end of 1939 and the start of the Second World
War, Britain had built 1,332,189 subsidized dwellings
through local housing authorities. The typical house had
three bedrooms and 700 to 800 square feet of floor area.
Almost all were two-story brick with tile or slate roofs.
Each had its own hot water system and was heated
(though an American would not so describe it) by the
typical British coal fire.

Mistakes were to be expected in the pioneering years
and mistakes were made. Too many local authorities covered large areas with small and monotonous houses, 12 to
the acre as prescribed by law. Site-planning was often mechanical in paper-planned geometric forms with little
regard for landscape. Too little provision was made for
stores, schools, inns, transportation, and other amenities.
The housing estates contained only one social class—the
poorest—and those living in public housing acquired
something of a social stigma.

All these faults were noted. Strenuous efforts to avoid
them have been made since World War II.

In Britain, new construction generally preceded slum
elimination. In fact, slum clearance did not become really
operative until the Housing Acts of 1930 and 1936 gave
local authorities strong powers to condemn areas of bad
housing and rebuild. The first of these important laws was

enacted by a minority Labor government with the support of all Parties, the second by a Conservative government.

It had been estimated that, out of 8 million houses in the whole country, 4.5 million were more than eighty years old. Much of the housing in the industrial towns, built between 1800 and 1850, was horribly congested (60–80 to the acre), insanitary, and overcrowded.[1]

The costs of slum clearance and rebuilding were of course much higher than the amounts required for building housing projects on vacant land. Moreover, housing authorities considered it desirable to rehouse as many families as possible in their old neighborhoods. For these reasons, the slums were replaced with apartments (or "blocks of flats," in the British terminology) instead of semi-detached or row houses. Most of the buildings were of five stories, without elevators. Planning and layout were poor at first and the projects were often like blocks of barracks in a sea of asphalt. Density was as high as 40 families to the acre. Unlike other Europeans and Americans, the British at that time had little tradition in apartment planning and design. But British architects gradually learned to make improvements. Trees, play spaces, communal laundries, and storage space came to be provided.

While the program fell far short of perfection in many details, its flaws should not obscure its solid achievement: Most cities in Britain had cleared and rebuilt their worst slums by the outbreak of World War II.

As local housing committees and their architects gained experience during the inter-war period, costs fell and

---

[1] [Mr. Bird's characterization of a density of "60–80 to the acre" as "horribly congested" sounds strange to American ears. See Chapter VIII. N. S.]

quality improved. *One of the most important lessons learned was that first cost was not so significant as first cost plus 40 years' maintenance. It was found that a higher first cost might often save money in the long run.*

Housing management became a respected profession. Candidates for training in this profession apply to the Society of Housing Managers or the Institute of Housing. An accepted applicant is assigned to the staff of a local housing authority as a student. During the intensely practical period of training, the student is paid a modest salary. The course, which lasts from two to three years, entitles the student at its completion to a housing manager's certificate of the Royal Institution of Chartered Surveyors.

The managers, mostly women, collect rents, report faults in equipment, show new tenants how to adapt themselves to life amid new conditions, and endeavor to promote good relations between tenant and landlord. They often become friendly counselors to the housewives, advising them on such things as the family budget. The highly trained women housing managers are very important in the success of British housing.

4

For several years following World War I, there was little construction of housing. A boom in private building, mostly by large scale speculators, began in 1923 when building costs fell. The houses were mostly for what we call "black-coated workers" and are called in America "white collar workers." The houses were built for sale, usually through 12- or 15-year loans from building societies.[1]

Since the speculative builders of private housing were interested in selling, not renting, their product was often shoddy. Flashy design and eye-catching gadgets were used to seduce the innocent buyer. The housing estates built by speculative builders were generally less well planned than those built by local housing authorities. Towns grew at random without proper planning. First-class market garden land was lost under a rash of houses. *However, overcrowding on narrow lots was prevented by the legal limit of 12 dwellings to the acre imposed on all new housing, private as well as public.*

Many of the larger builders, believing that a body of satisfied customers would be a long-term asset, were concerned about the operations of some of the build-and-run speculators. To discourage activities which tended to reflect unfavorably on the whole industry, the better firms organized the National House Builders' Registration Council which drafted minimum standards for house construction. All the members of the Council pledged compliance and the government gave its approval.

Early in World War II the magnitude of the post-war housing problem was realized. The Churchill government took steps throughout the War to prepare for the peace-

---

[1] These societies do not themselves build. Their lending is closely regulated by law to protect the borrower. For example, a building society cannot foreclose except for default and the borrower must then be credited in full for all payments made. Building societies are an important feature of British building finance.

time need.[1] A Postwar Building Department was set up in the Ministry of Works to study construction methods, especially those developed during the War, which were applicable to housing. The government also created the Ministry of Town and Country Planning [2] to organize land use and building development after the War. During the War the Ministry of Health prepared a new official "Housing Manual" for public housing which was published by the Churchill government in 1944.

When the Labor Party for the first time won a clear majority in the 1945 Parliamentary election, the Churchill government had already provided the groundwork for a post-war building program to meet the acute housing shortage. The only housing issues during the 1945 campaign were how quickly one million dwellings could be provided, and by what methods. The Conservative Party recommended a combination of private and public enterprise, as before the War. The Labor Party favored reliance on public housing. With the victory of Labor, its program was adopted.

Remembering the inflation that followed World War I, the government kept the wartime system of licensing and price control in effect for all building as well as for remodeling and repairs. All post-war construction has been restricted to essential factories, housing, schools, and war damage repairs. Virtually no other building has been permitted. As of May, 1951, these restrictions still exist. The ratio of licenses for public and private housing was set at

---

[1] The writer remembers the disturbance caused at a committee meeting of housing technicians by the rather too close arrival of a flying bomb.

[2] Since January, 1951, renamed the "Ministry of Local Government and Planning" and given control of housing.

4 to 1. That is, only one dwelling could be built by private enterprise for every four built by local authorities.

To stretch the available supply of building labor and building materials, dwelling units built by private enterprise were limited to a maximum floor area of 1000 square feet (increased to 1500 square feet in 1949). Moreover, construction costs of private housing were not permitted to exceed those of comparable homes built by local authorities in the same neighborhood.

Building enterprise has thus been prevented from using up scarce building materials and the precious man-hours of building workers to produce mansions. The government's policy has been to house first the working class, particularly the homeless veterans with young families. More than half a million new dwellings have been provided by local housing authorities. Another half a million families have been taken care of in temporary housing and by the conversion into apartments of old buildings.

American readers, many of whom are accustomed to thinking that the know-how of private enterprise is sufficient to solve every problem, may raise one or both eyebrows at this account of British post-war difficulties and the measures taken to resolve them. The role of the government in Britain has been exactly the reverse of the government's role in America. This is because the British people have long been in agreement that good housing for ordinary people is a national necessity. The need to build a better Britain after the War was urged in countless speeches, pamphlets, and books by statesmen of all shades of opinion. We took these promises literally and we have proceeded to carry them out. *No responsible spokesman for any political party has questioned the assumption that local housing authorities must have a large share in the task.*

5

When the War ended there were great hopes that pre-fabrication would make a real contribution to housing by employing the engineering and aircraft industries to supplement the capacity of the building industry. The lead towards prefabrication given by the Churchill government was actively followed by architects, builders, and industrialists who devoted much thought, experiment, and finance to it.

From the outset two kinds of prefabricated house were envisaged. The first was a temporary house for blitzed areas and for vacant land in towns and villages. The Ministry of Works designed a heating, hot water, and plumbing unit for quantity production; it has proved excellent in service. House shells were built of aluminum, steel, asbestos-cement, and cast concrete (lumber is a relatively expensive imported commodity) according to the character of the manufacturing firm. The houses were intended to last and be used for only ten years, though it is now clear they will be needed much longer and will survive. The temporary house program has ended after 160,000 have been provided.

The second kind of prefab is a permanent two-story building designed to last the 60-year loan period of the traditional brick house. Space and equipment standards are the same.

For both temporary and permanent prefabricated houses the procedure has been for the manufacturer to submit designs to the Ministry of Works. After rigorous tests and studies of first cost, maintenance cost, heat and sound insulations, fire resistance, freedom from risk of vermin, and availability of materials, an approved house gets special facilities for manufacture. The Ministry has approved about a dozen such prefabricated types of dwellings, from which housing authorities may choose.

Prefabricated houses have lightened the post-war burden on the regular building industry. But they have rarely proved cheaper than the traditional brick house. Some of the temporary prefabs, in fact, were more expensive than the larger and permanent brick houses. Housing authorities have become cool toward prefabs and the demand for them has dropped steadily as the regular building industry has increased production.

One cannot drive away houses like finished cars. At the end of the assembly line, the expense of the automobile to the purchaser is likewise ended. At the end of the assembly line a local housing authority as buyer of the prefab house, must still reckon with the cost of foundations, sewerage connections, roads, landscaping, etc.[1]

What the housing experts are now looking for with the enthusiastic support of the Ministry of Works, is methods of speeding up and simplifying *traditional* construction, using mechanical equipment and semi-skilled labor. Factories are producing more and more subassemblies such

---

[1] Prefabricated houses are not yet available for purchase by private buyers.

as doors with frames, whole staircases, windows with glazing, roof sections, and kitchen equipment. Much site work that cannot be transferred to the factory is taken care of by the bulldozer, trench digger, and road layer. To supplement brick building, walls are cast in insulating concrete by unskilled labor.

In 1950 the research director in the Ministry of Works, Mr. R. Fitzmaurice, pointed out that new methods had not yet achieved very much. The outer shell of a house represents only one-third of the total cost, he said, and the great need is an adaptable prefabricated inside which could be surrounded by walls and roof of any convenient permanent material, such as brick. It must never be forgotten that heating, plumbing, electrical assemblies, and interior finishing represent a high proportion of the total cost. Therefore, the search for a prefabricated inside appears to be a sound objective.

Prefabrication is not dead in Britain but is changing its nature. The original idea that the shell of the house could be mass-produced in factories as easily and cheaply as automobiles has proved false. The trend now is toward a merger of prefabrication with traditional construction to achieve good houses at low cost by any method—mechanical or hand, in the factory or on the site.

6

The British house has grown about 25% in size since the War. The normal three-bedroom house of 1939 was

required by the Ministry of Health to have 700 to 800
square feet. The figure in 1950 is 900 to 950 square feet.
The 1949 "Housing Manual" prescribes schedules for public housing ranging from 750 to 800 square feet for two-
bedroom houses up to 1100 to 1175 square feet for four-
bedroom dwellings.

More attention is being paid to insulation, to save heat
and reduce noise. The steep rise in fuel cost since the War
has made us conscious of the need of adequate insulation
and its use is growing as in the United States. A new type
of heating unit is centrally placed so that it gives in the
living room the open fire beloved by the British as a focus
of glow in their cloudy climate, provides the hot water,
and supplies some heat to the rest of the house.

Local housing authorities are free to plan houses according to local ways of living provided they comply with
the minimum floor area requirements and other basic
standards of the Ministry of Health. There is no bureaucratic control of design.

Perhaps the most notable *new* feature of British housing
is concern with town and country planning, including land
utilization in its broadest sense. During World War II
three select government committees (appointed by the
Chamberlain government just before the War) developed
the broad outlines of a new policy. Their recommendations became effective with the passage of the Town and
Country Planning Act of 1947. This Act has teeth to enable planning authorities to translate paper plans into
streets, housing, parks, and other amenities. Public housing estates are no longer placed casually where the local
housing authority can readily buy land. Instead, the housing estates are located so as to form integral parts of the

planned development of the entire area. The main intention is that towns shall grow in an orderly manner and not haphazard as before.

In 1949, Parliament extended the powers of housing authorities beyond the field of working class housing, what is called in the United States "housing for low-income families." Local authorities are now empowered to build for *all* classes of the community and also have broad powers to make available on land acquired by them, sites for privately built houses, stores, churches, inns, gas stations, and other enterprises.

Matching the new concern with overall planning is the attention being given to the architectural grouping and site plan of every housing scheme. The purely geometrical layout has gone. Every advantage is taken of such natural features as streams, slopes, and fine old trees. When the site is flat and treeless, buildings are grouped in pleasant forms and trees are planted. Row houses (or "terraces," as they are called), semi-detached houses, apartments of varying heights, and single-story houses for old people are arranged in groups, many of them about open greens. Not every project is beautiful. But the Ministry of Health is using precept and gentle pressure to prod the unimaginative and backward local authorities. The current objective is to serve the needs of the whole population in a balanced way, catering not only to the average family of three or four but, also, to very small and very large families, single persons, and aged couples in a variety of plan arrangements.

The idea of the complete neighborhood has taken hold. Housing is being built in planned relation to schools, stores, churches, community centers, and other facilities.

These are termed "neighborhood units," a basic idea being to encourage neighborly feeling and civic consciousness. Reams of statistics have been prepared on the right ratio of homes to each type of store, how far children of various ages should walk to what types of schools, and so on. No site planner need ever feel lonely for lack of figures.

7

The next logical step from the neighborhood unit is the planning of a complete new town with its own business and shopping center, its own industries, and a number of neighborhood units. The state-sponsored New Towns, of which two dozen are building or projected, are the most striking feature of post-war British housing policy.

This bold experiment envisages the planning and building of these new towns for a population of 30,000 to 50,000 each. These self-sufficient new towns are the main instruments in the national policy of planned decentralization from congested urban areas. The primary purpose is to thin out the old industrial areas, especially London. Each new town is linked with an old, overcrowded area in a city. The eight new towns in the Greater London region are expected to house a population of something over one-quarter of a million persons.[1]

---

[1] Other new towns are being built in the principal industrial areas to relieve congestion in the old towns. Several city housing authorities are providing a portion of their housing in the form of more or less self-contained satellite communities.

*Each new town is built by a government-financed de-
velopment corporation which has power to acquire the
land needed for the new town. The American TVA is ad-
mittedly the model for this type of public administrative
body. When the job is done, the town will be handed over
to an elected municipal council and its permanent officials.*

Although the new towns will be in a sense garden cities,
Sir Ebenezer Howard's idea of a purely garden community
has been modified and the towns will include also apartment blocks. Firms with obsolescent plants and no room
to expand are given encouragement and facilities to move
to a new town, taking their workers along. Houses for the
firms' workers are provided by the development corporation and the government gives other assistance. The new
communities are to be truly *towns*, not garden suburbs.[1]

In all this housing and planning work there is the over-
riding question of density—the number of dwellings per
acre. The original limit of 12 families to the acre has been
abandoned for a more flexible system. When a newly built
neighborhood offers complete communal facilities, the
gross density may range from 30 to 40 persons per acre.
When a congested area is redeveloped, the density may go
up to 60 persons per acre.

Net density is that of the housing project only. The
Ministry of Health allows great flexibility in net density to
suit local needs, but talks in terms of 35 habitable rooms [2]
(6 to 11 families) per acre for new suburban neighbor-

---

[1] Sir Ebenezer Howard, born one hundred years ago, is affectionately
referred to in current housing literature as "the father of the garden city
and the grandfather of the new towns."

[2] The normal three-bedroom house has five habitable rooms. The
smallest two-bedroom house has three habitable rooms. A four-bedroom
house has six habitable rooms. Houses of different size are often mixed
together in the same block or group.

hoods and of 100 to 120 (20 to 35 families) for redeveloped inner areas. In redevelopment, the Ministry favors a mixture of eight- and three-story apartment houses and row houses. Barracks of uniform height are frowned upon.

Over three decades, British housing thought has progressed gradually from the elementary idea of providing some cheap homes for the poor to the concept of a national service supplying pleasant dwellings to families of all income levels. At first it was thought that anyone could design a working class cottage and in many cases anyone did so, hardly excluding the municipal engineer's office boy. Few architects were interested in public housing and fewer still understood the technique of economical house design. But as public housing grew the architects moved in. Many local authorities now employ a full-time architectural staff.

British architects exchange experience and opinion with continental architects interested in public housing, notably those in the Scandinavian countries, the Netherlands, and Switzerland. This co-operation is much closer than that between American and British architects.

8

Despite the building boom, there is still a housing shortage. New construction has made up for the 218,000 homes totally destroyed by bombing and the million or more seriously damaged. But the steady increase in small families and the movement and expansion of industry have maintained severe shortages in many urban areas.[1] The white collar workers, some of whom prefer to buy or build houses larger than the local authority dwellings, represent a large unsatisfied demand.

The continuing shortage is a great hindrance to mobility of labor, particularly of the higher technicians and managerial class. Employers who want new employees can get them if houses are available—otherwise the chances are poor. Because housing is such an important factor in Britain's industrial recovery, it holds a high position in the building priority list.

Beyond fulfillment of the immediate demand for shelter is the problem of the remaining slums. This cannot be tackled until there is a surplus of new dwellings into which the slum families can move. The people of Britain know that neighborhoods characterized by row upon row of dirty, obsolescent dwellings on traffic-laden streets take a steady toll of child life, because the children have nowhere else to play. The government, with full popular approval, is planning toward eventual redevelopment of blighted areas, even where the buildings are reasonably sanitary, but where there is overcrowding, insufficient open space, or a lack of trees and green.

The British people today are well posted on housing and think a great deal about it. The two Wars have been partly responsible for their education. There is a realization that a great many British homes are simply not good enough for a modern democracy in an age of technical advance. Further, the influence of housing on the nation's

---

[1] There is a strong tendency for younger marriages since the War, hence the maintenance of housing demand. Leaders of the Labor Party say their full employment policy is responsible for this!

physical and emotional health is understood. A well-housed family is a clean and healthy family, and the man with a good house is not inclined toward revolution. On Saturday afternoons he is more interested in his garden than in a street brawl.

Individuals and political parties will, doubtless, continue to differ on the best means for achieving good housing for all—but no one questions the objective. Differences are confined to such details as the proportionate role of public and private enterprise. *There is no likelihood that any government, be it Conservative, Liberal, or Labor, will change the direction of British housing policy, which is firmly set on the path of rebuilding Britain, so that there will be good housing and comfortable living conditions for every British family.*

XI. *The Housing Act of 1949—and Your Community*

BY

Lee F. Johnson

[Lee F. Johnson was Assistant Administrator of the United States Housing Authority from 1938 to 1944, when that Federal agency was formulating the principles and policies of the first permanent public housing program in the history of the country. He resigned in 1944 to become the Executive Vice President of the National Public Housing Conference (now the National Housing Conference).

[As the chief administrative officer of the organization which has been the spearhead of the public housing movement, he has rendered unique service. To him is due much of the credit for unifying and thus making effective the work of labor, veteran groups, and civic betterment associations throughout the country, which culminated in the passage of the Housing Act of 1949. Lee Johnson, with little funds and a tiny staff, led the forces of good government to victory over the opposition of powerful vested interests.

[In 1950, Mr. Johnson received the University of Colorado's Recognition Medal "for distinguished service in public housing."]

1

THE HOUSING ACT of 1949 gives American cities and towns an opportunity to provide good housing and rebuild decayed neighborhoods. The low-rent housing section provides for approximately 810,000 dwellings, six times more houses than were built under the pioneer U. S. Housing Act of 1937. This is the first large-scale attack on the slums. Yet the slums are so numerous that 810,000 new dwellings would shelter only one-seventh of the estimated six million urban families who are now in bad housing.

Congress defined the purpose of the Act in these words:

"The Congress hereby declares that the general welfare and security of the Nation and the health and living standards of its people require housing production and related community development sufficient to remedy the serious housing shortage, the elimination of substandard and other inadequate housing through the clearance of slums and blighted areas, and the realization as soon as feasible of the goal of a decent home and suitable living environment for every American family, thus contributing to the development of communities and to the advancement of the growth, wealth, and security of the Nation."

This was also the philosophy of the United States Housing Act of 1937. Until that year the United States, almost alone among the more advanced nations, had persisted in treating the slums as a problem of private enterprise, subject to local regulation. When a century of experience proved that the slum areas in most American communities were growing instead of disappearing—the Federal government finally intervened. The Housing Act of 1937, as amended in 1938, authorized $800 million in Federal loans and up to $28 million in annual subsidies for low-rent housing.

Federal housing activities were brought together by the Housing Act of 1949 under one new Federal department: the Housing and Home Finance Agency. The two chief constituents of this Agency are the *Federal Housing Administration,* which insures housing mortgages and the *Public Housing Administration,* which supervises the low-rent housing program of local housing authorities throughout the nation.

The 1949 Act has six titles:

Title I provides for redevelopment of blighted urban areas, to be financed over a five-year period by $1 billion in Federal loans to cities and $500 million in capital grants. Cities may borrow for planning and temporary financing, repaying the loans when the land is sold or leased for redevelopment. Since blighted areas are generally in the heart of the city and are correspondingly expensive, the Act provides capital grants to cover two-thirds of the loss suffered by the city in clearing slum property. One-third of such loss must be met by the city—but the Federal government makes this as painless as possible by allowing the city to include as part of its contribution the value of parks, schools, streets, utilities, or other city improvements. The city may also include as part of its share the value of the manpower needed to clear the site.

Federal loans (but no capital grants) may also be had by localities for developing vacant land.

Title II was an emergency section providing extensions for certain FHA insurance authorizations expiring in August 1949.

Title III, providing low-rent housing, was the crux of the fight in Congress. It amended the Housing Act of 1937 by authorizing loans and subsidies for approximately 810,-000 locally built low-rent dwellings. The Public Housing Administration may empower local housing authorities to start 135,000 dwellings each year. The President may, however, step up the program to 200,000 or reduce it to 50,000 if the Council of Economic Advisers recommends expansion or contraction in the public interest.[1]

Title IV authorized the administrator of the Housing and Home Finance Agency to carry on technical research and other studies to help lower construction costs and increase the production of housing. Research may be undertaken co-operatively with industry, labor, state and local governments, educational institutions, and other nonprofit organizations.

Title V authorized the Secretary of Agriculture to give financial assistance to farm owners in building, improving, or repairing farm structures.

Title VI required the census director to take a housing census in 1950 and every succeeding decade.

---

[1] That was the intent of the law. The real estate lobby has not despaired, however, of amending the Act to reduce the number of new dwellings below even 50,000 units.

2

How does the Housing Act of 1949 affect you, as a citizen? Whether you are the mayor, a councilman, a teacher, a lawyer, an architect, a minister, a union official, a club leader, a merchant—or merely a voter in search of facts, the first thing to understand is that nothing will happen unless your community acts. The Federal government is not going to ship a few trainloads of prefabricated houses or any other kind of houses into your city. The Federal government is not going to persuade you to build low-rent dwellings and clean up your blighted areas. Your own city must take the initiative.

The most vigorous and effective attacks on the slums have been made where alert citizens' organizations have co-operated with a progressive local housing authority and a sympathetic city administration. In short, public housing is no accident. It takes planning. Most of all it takes determination. You cannot get low-rent housing in your city unless you are willing to fight for it.

Let us assume that you have a normal dislike for needless misery and a normal disgust with slums. You want to use the Housing Act of 1949 to make your town a better place to live in. What can you do?

The first step is to put yourself in a position where your voice will count. As a solitary citizen you can write a letter or talk to a public official. Your vocal chords will have no more decibels than any other cry in the wilderness.

How can you make your voice heard? Only through organization. That cry may be the beginning of democracy at work.

The organization may be a club or a business group or a labor union or a church group. Best of all it may be a housing association which undertakes to represent all of the key civic organizations for betterment of housing in your community.

The policy of the housing association, or any similar organization, might be stated as follows:

"We care a great deal about the future of our city. We believe that good housing is basic for the health of the community. We want our local government to utilize the funds and powers available under the Housing Act of 1949 to clear out slum areas and to provide healthful low-rent homes for low-income families. We will support our public officials on sound housing policies and help them override sniping from selfish interests. We will oppose policies that are shortsighted and harmful. We will make suggestions and work for their adoption. We will vote for city officials whose active interest in betterment of housing conditions makes them deserving of our support and we will endeavor to influence other voters to make similar effective use of the ballot."

What next?

1. If your community does not have a local housing authority see that one is authorized by the city council and promptly appointed.[1]

A local housing authority usually consists of five unpaid

---

[1] A special ordinance will probably be necessary. Technical advice on this and other problems may be had from the Public Housing Administration, Washington 25, D. C.

citizens, named by the mayor. The men and women appointed as the local authority should represent the whole community—not just the businessmen or the real estate men or the labor leaders. The local authority bears the responsibility for inaugurating and guiding the entire program of urban redevelopment and housing. Until a local housing authority has been appointed, your city cannot talk business with the Federal government.

2. If your community does have a local housing authority as many cities do, get acquainted with its program. Find out what has been accomplished. Visit the housing projects that have been built and decide whether or not you like them.

Get complete and specific facts on the projects being planned under the 1949 Act. How many dwelling units will there be? Are most of them planned for vacant land so the housing shortage will not be further aggravated by the premature demolition of slums? Is the population density of the new projects low enough to avoid overcrowding with all its attendant evils? Are there self-contained parks and playgrounds? Are the projects so located and designed as to give promise of becoming, not future slums, but permanent community assets?

You should make careful inquiries as to the housing authority's policy on racial segregation. Many housing authorities in northern cities that accepted segregation as normal or unavoidable in 1940, are now faced with state laws that have compelled a change of policy. In some instances local authorities have discovered that interracial living means *less* friction and they are therefore planning complete integration. As a citizen, you have a voice in determining how your local housing authority can best provide for all of the people of your community regardless of race, creed, or color.

3. Since there is no substitute for direct observation, any citizen who is concerned with housing conditions should visit slum housing, become acquainted with the people who live there, and inspect the rooms, kitchens, and the toilet facilities. The interested citizen should endeavor to find out how many persons sleep in one room and how much of the family income goes for rent.

If he (or she) cares to pursue investigations further, it will prove very enlightening to find out who owns the slums. Many of those who cry out loudest against "socialized public housing" will be discovered to have a financial interest in the operation of slum properties.

To sum up: It is the responsibility of intelligent citizens interested in the betterment of living conditions to make personal investigation. Such inquiries will provide facts to answer critics of public housing who keep repeating, "Let private enterprise do the job." It will not take much investigation to prove that, in the field of housing for low-income families, private enterprise has failed.

3

_____

The mechanics of the public housing section of the 1949 Act are much like the procedure under the United States Housing Act of 1937. The local housing authority applies to the Public Housing Administration for a "reservation" of a specified number of dwelling units, based on an estimate of need. The PHA may then issue a program reservation, which means that if the housing is economically and soundly planned PHA will later make a contract for financial aid.

The local housing authority may also apply for a preliminary loan to be used for studies of housing need and possible sites as well as for appraisals, options, surveys, preparation of preliminary plans, and administrative overhead. An application to the Federal government for a preliminary loan cannot be forwarded to Washington before it is approved by the local city council or governing body of the community.

Next the local authority engages architects and hires other staff members to handle the design and construction of the projected housing. The Federal government makes a contract for financial aid provided that (1) the local government has granted tax exemption, (2) the local authority agrees to raise at least 10% of total development cost from private investors, and (3) the local authority has made sure that its dwellings will not compete with acceptable private housing.

Upon execution of the Federal contract, the local authority proceeds to build. Sites are usually acquired through negotiation with private owners, but condemnation may be used. It is the local authority's responsibility to help displaced families find other quarters. Contracts are awarded through open bidding; funds for construction are borrowed privately on a short-term basis. When construction is about 40% complete, the authority sells long-term bonds to pay off its short-term obligations. PHA stands ready to buy up to 90% of these bonds but rarely does so because local authorities find that they can borrow at lower interest rates by selling their bonds to institutions and private investors. These bonds are exempt from Federal income taxes.

The Housing Act limits the cost of construction and dwelling equipment to $1,750 a room (except that in special cases the ceiling may be raised to $2,500). *Past experience in public housing has shown that buildings costing more at the start often prove cheaper in the end.*[1]

4

The great bulk of the cost of public housing is met by the tenants themselves. Low-income families often pay as much as 80% of the total monthly cost. However, part of the cost—the rent—is met by government subsidies. There are two such subsidies or grants, one from the Federal government and the other from the city or town.

The local subsidy is in the form of exemption of the housing project from local real estate taxes. The community gets back as a substitute a payment amounting to about 10% of the shelter rent. In general, these payments by local housing authorities into the city treasury are more than the taxes previously assessed against the site, but they amount to only from 25% to 30% of the tax on other modern housing. To say that the city gives up nothing and

[1] For example, Detroit spent $158,472 extra to provide central coal heat instead of individual gas heating for 1,704 dwellings and thereby saved $40,896 a year—a total of $2,453,760 for the 60-year life of the project.

gains in the process is the truth. The cost to the city of needless disease, juvenile delinquency, and other concealed costs of the slums makes up many times over for the small tax concession granted to low-rent public housing.[1]

The Federal subsidy is flexible and varies from year to year. It is just enough to cover the difference between the annual cost of housing (after deduction of the local subsidy) and what the tenant can afford to pay. Since rents in public housing are scaled in proportion to family income and have no relation to the number of rooms, this means that in good times rents are higher and only a small portion of the subsidy is needed. But if, in a depression, tenant incomes should fall, rents would go down, too, and more or all of the subsidy might be required.[2]

The subsidy serves two purposes. First, it lowers rents. Second, it secures the bonds issued by the local housing authority. The Federal commitment enables the local authority to borrow at very low interest rates and the saving on interest means lower rents. Local housing authority bonds are in the portfolios of leading banks, trust companies, and other private investors.

The Federal and local subsidies alone do not explain the ability of a local housing authority to rent for $20 or $30 a standard dwelling that would cost $60 to $80 if privately owned. There are several additional reasons. One is that the local housing authority makes no profit. In slum prop-

---

[1] See Chapter II for facts on the cost of slums to the city government.

[2] The Housing Act limits the annual subsidy to about 3½% of the total cost of developing the project. For example, with an average dwelling cost of $10,000, the maximum subsidy would be $350 a year or $29.16 a month for each apartment. The subsidy is payable for forty years. Under the 1937 Housing Act, the Federal government's annual contributions have been less than 60% of the maximum allowed.

erties, a profit of 25% to 35% per annum is common. Another reason is that cost of capital is low because bonds of
the local housing authority—safe, secure, and exempt
from personal income tax—are readily sold to private and
institutional investors at very low interest rates. Cost of
operation is also held to a minimum, partly through expert
planning of the projects and partly through the co-operation of tenants who give generously of their own time and
energy for maintaining many of the public housing projects. Last—but by no means of least importance—the
losses from "vacancies" and "uncollected rent" are only
about one-fourth of one per cent compared to an average
of about 10% in private rental housing.

Low-rent public housing may be occupied only by families whose net annual income at the time of admission
(plus $100 exemption for each minor child) does not ex-
ceed five times the annual rent. For example, if the rent—
including utilities—were $25 a month or $300 a year, the
income limit for a family with three minor children would
be $1,800.

5

The most consistent and effective enemy of public housing in recent years has been Representative Jesse Wolcott
(R., Michigan). In 1948 he prevented enactment of a
housing bill. In 1949 he tried again, closing his argument
with this warning: "No one argues that there is anything
in this bill for any locality outside of ten metropolitan

areas. If any of you who live in cities with populations of from 20,000 up to 500,000 think there is anything in this bill for your people, read it over and become disillusioned. You are not going to get any of the benefits, until and unless this program is multiplied at least ten times."

Mr. Wolcott was not within hailing distance of the truth. More than half of the cities participating in the slum clearance and public housing program have populations of less than 20,000.

The Housing Act of 1949 is a tool for every American community. It is meant for small towns as well as great cities. It is designed to help any community make a real start in providing decent housing in place of slums. If you think your town has no slums, take a second look.

For a decade the well-financed real estate lobby was able to prevent all Federal aid for slum clearance or to provide healthful, livable housing for low-income families. At last, in 1949, a powerful array of citizens' organizations succeeded in forcing the housing bill out of committee where it had been kept bottled up by the lobby. A few months thereafter victory was finally achieved, as a result of co-operation and teamwork of enlightened public-spirited citizens.

Immediately after the Housing Act of 1949 became law, the real estate lobby boldly announced that it would fight public housing in every community. This is a desperate attempt to veto legislation enacted by public demand. However, the determination and the potency of the reactionary lobby should not be minimized.

With millions of dollars for newspaper advertisements, radio programs, literature, and professional organizers, they have won more than half of the local referenda which they have forced on the public housing issue. The methods used are sometimes dangerously un-American. In Denver and elsewhere, for example, they adopted a questionnaire technique. Agents of the lobby asked residents of areas chosen for new housing projects what they thought of the plan and solicited signatures for petitions opposing use of the site chosen. If the family seemed unwilling to sign, the agent pointed out that certain "undesirable" persons—i.e., Negroes or Mexican-Americans—would be eligible for public housing and would therefore become neighbors of the established residents. The racist argument, slyly used, often clinched a signature.

This type of campaign is no accident. A complete set of instructions for an assault on public housing at the local level has been distributed to its members by the National Association of Home Builders. The material was mailed in 1949 and 1950 above the signatures of Rodney M. Lockwood, president of NAHB, and John M. Dickerman, legislative director. Here is a sample of the instructions from a pamphlet entitled *Public Housing on a Community Level.*

"Insist upon full public disclosure of exactly where this public housing will be located. Prepare a map of the site and surrounding area within a radius of one to two miles. Contact the existing organized protective associations, taxpayers' associations, community clubs, and similar organizations which have been established to preserve property values of single-family homes in that area. Point out to the officers of these groups the threat to the value of their properties in the areas where such public housing will be erected. *As Federally subsidized units, the normal and customary occupancy requirements will obviously not apply nor be enforceable.* Home owners and parents are naturally quite interested in not only the preservation of property values but in *the type of community in which their children will be raised and in which they will live.*" [1]

Advice on the technique of defeating public housing includes the recommendation that a front organization be set up and named the "Home Owners' Protective Association" or "Taxpayers' Protective Association" if no suitable existing organization is willing to lend itself to the scheme. The confidential instructions emphasize, however, that if a respectable organization can be persuaded to act as a mouthpiece for the lobby that is the best technique. The local agents of the lobby are advised to use such smear words as "political" and "socialized" public housing. They are to insist that "private enterprise can do the job," "public housing costs more to build than private housing," "public housing increases property taxes" and so on.

Five successive steps to block public housing are recommended. Whenever a local housing authority applies to the Public Housing Administration for a program reservation, the lobby advises its local agents to:

1. Organize to block approval in the city council.

2. If this move fails, get signatures to a petition for a referendum to veto the council's action.

3. If that fails, file a taxpayer's suit to enjoin the local authority from proceeding with the program.

4. If all three strategems fail, harass the local authority with opposition to its choice of sites, especially those on vacant land.

5. Seek amendments to state housing laws to require a local referendum whenever a housing authority seeks city council approval for a new development.

---

[1] Emphasis supplied.

The National Association of Home Builders is only one part of the lobby. Its principal partners in the local battle are the National Association of Real Estate Boards and the United States Savings and Loan League. Behind this junta stand the even more powerful Mortgage Bankers Association of America, United States Chamber of Commerce, and Producers Council.

To a greater or lesser extent the enormous wealth of this lobby touches every community in the land. The local real estate board and the owners of the local slums have a loose but obvious business relationship with the banks and financial institutions that hold mortgages on slum property. The local bank in all probability is a depository of funds of the local department stores. Under these circumstances, the publisher and editor of the town *Clarion* must be men of unusual courage—not to speak of financial strength—if the newspaper is to support public housing. In your city, as in every other community, reactionary real estate and financial interests, under the general guidance of the national lobby, will burrow from within to block public housing.

That is why citizens should organize. It was citizen organization that finally crushed the lobby in Congress. Now that the lobby has shifted the battleground to the communities, citizens should be prepared to fight in their own towns. They should give unstinted support to honest and farseeing public officials. They should stand up against the public officials who would sell out to the lobbyists. Nothing short of militant action by organized voters will enable American cities to *use* the 1949 Housing Act for the rebuilding of the cities of our nation.

XII. *The Segregation Threat in Housing*

BY

Charles Abrams

[Charles Abrams is a pioneer in the long fight for improvement of housing conditions in America. He was instrumental in writing the model state statute on public housing and the laws which created the first local housing authority in America.

[In recognition of his services, Mr. Abrams was appointed as the first counsel to the New York City Housing Authority under the administration of Mayor LaGuardia. He thus participated in framing basic policies in public housing, helped establish the initial administrative procedures, and defended the constitutionality of public housing in the courts.

[Mr. Abrams is the author of *Revolution in Land* (1939) and *The Future of Housing* (1946). In recent years he has lectured widely at universities and is Chairman of the Housing and Planning Division of the New School for Social Research.]

1

IF AMERICA meets its minimum housing needs it must build new housing equal to half its pre-war supply by 1965. The bulk of these new homes will be built with some kind of government aid.[1] The construction will be so great that it will involve demolition of large areas of obsolete but nevertheless inhabited buildings. Millions of families will be forced to move from their present homes, the racial composition of our neighborhoods will be recast. While the program is being carried out in the name of neighborhood improvement and civic betterment, little thought has been given to the plight of the human beings affected, so many of whom are members of minority groups.

In some cities, public housing on vacant land is providing good housing for the displaced minorities. But in others, masses of them, particularly Negroes, Mexicans, and Puerto Ricans are being shifted, hemmed in, shunted about, crowded in with others, ousted from slum to slum, only to be pushed about again like pariahs. This is being done under popular labels like "public works," "slum clearance," or "urban redevelopment." The illusion exists that the way to get rid of slums is to tear them down with little or no concern about the people who live in them. The new fashion in slum clearance is to throw the baby out with the bath water.

---

[1] Almost three-quarters of all private apartment buildings in 1949 were made possible by Federal insurance of the risks. In 1942, the National Housing Agency's participation directly or indirectly in home indebtedness was 57%, i.e., through FHA, members of the Home Loan Banks and the Home Owners Loan Corporation. Public housing operations for slum-dwellers has scheduled building of 810,000 units. In ten states Federal public housing aid has been supplemented by state or local programs. The New York City Housing Authority, the most advanced in the program, was doing 42% of all the housing construction in the city in 1949—before the Korean crisis.

Simultaneously, a great urban redevelopment program has been launched under which initial Federal subsidies of a half a billion and a billion dollars in loans will make it possible to clear slum sites of their occupants. The cleared land will then be sold.

The housing reformer who should be a protector of minorities has been numbed into acquiescence by the momentum of the very reforms he himself launched. Having made slum clearance a goal, he now finds it hard to condemn it as an evil.

The hovels these minorities live in might have been torn down years ago when vacancies were plentiful. They might be torn down in the future if and when other housing may be available to the occupants. But now, bad as the slums are, they provide at least some protection against the elements. They are better than a park bench or the "hotbeds" to which these people are being consigned. The plight of these homeless Americans is becoming one of the country's top social problems.

The new private suburban developments will not accept the displaced minorities. Neither will the private urban redevelopment projects. In public housing, where these families could be sheltered, less than half are eligible and less than a third of these can ever hope to be accepted. Many are either non-citizens, or their families are too large or too small. Others drift away when their homes are torn down. To make matters worse, the slum sites on which some of these minorities have their homes are being deliberately marked out for new streets, highways, and parking facilities.

Hundreds of thousands of these families crowd into remaining slums, putting up bonuses for the privilege of a room or two, paying rents that hardly leave enough for subsistence. Overcrowding for minorities is four times as severe for non-whites as for whites, the proportion of substandard housing six times as great.

Public officials have also failed to see the social implications that must result from this recasting of the social and racial compositions of our neighborhoods. Segregated neighborhoods mean not only segregated housing but segregated schools, playgrounds, and social facilities. Zoning individuals into compartments determined by color is a process which eliminates opportunity for a fusion of interests. Confining children to separate facilities sharpens the lines of distinction and develops illusions of superiority and inferiority. Natural distinctions are converted into priorities and color or racial differences deteriorate into social differences. Once rooted in housing, the segregation pattern will spread unarrested until the ghetto becomes part of the American landscape, sanctioned not only by custom but enforced by law. The background and reasons for the development of this menacing pattern is therefore of major concern to American democracy.

2

Before the great housing shortage for minorities, Negroes and whites, Jews and gentiles, Italians and Poles lived in the same general area. Their neighborhoods were ghettos, but they were voluntary ghettos held together by common cultural and social ties. Though social maladjustment was the by-product, the old slum-ghetto had the saving grace that it was a product of choice more than compulsion. The era was one in which social patterns were fluid and class lines elastic. Individuals moved from one neighborhood to another more or less as they pleased, migrating into the better neighborhoods as they improved their circumstances.

Distances between home and place of work were then measured in furlongs and limited by a horse's endurance, so that employee and boss, mistress and servant, tradesman and customer, all lived in the same neighborhood, albeit their living standards differed. The minorities had to live nearby to serve their financial betters, launder their collars and cuffs, bake their bread, trim their sideburns. Their presence undermined neither the social status of their more fortunate neighbors nor their real estate investments. Indeed, it was fashionable for the mansion folk to have their Negro servants live nearby, if not in the house itself.[1] Mere presence of a minority, *per se*, did not disturb social status or affect neighborhood values.

Thus, a composite and mixed, if not yet a blended society, made it possible for people of all races, creeds, classes, types, and social positions to live nearby and to emulate their betters; to mingle in the same coffeehouses and theatres, if they could afford them; to browse in the same libraries or attend the same forums; to have their children play in the same parks and attend the same schools; to live in and enjoy an environment which facilitated social improvement and assimilation rather than class stratification or fancied aristocracy based upon race and color.

Up to the closing of the frontier and during the early stages of American capitalism, the line between the upper

---

[1] This, in fact, is the origin of the "alley dwellings," little shacks crowded in back of the mansion and out of sight of the street, which still plague Baltimore, Washington, D. C., and other cities.

and lower crusts was a narrow one. In 1861, Abraham Lincoln could still describe America as a land where most were neither employers nor workers and where the hired workers were not permanently moored to any fixed condition of life. "Men with their families—wives, sons, and daughters—work for themselves, on their farms, in their houses, and in their shops, taking the whole product to themselves, and asking no favors of capital on the one hand, nor of hired laborers or slaves on the other. . . . The prudent, penniless beginner in the world labors for wages for awhile, saves a surplus with which to buy tools or land for himself, then labors on his own account another while, and at length hires another new beginner to help him. This is the just and generous and prosperous system which opens the way to all—gives hope to all, and consequent energy and progress and improvement of condition to all." [1]

3

With the end of the Civil War and the vast influx of immigrants from abroad, there was every indication that a healthy levelling of social differences was to become America's heritage—in the words of Benjamin Franklin, "a general happy mediocrity," with no great gulfs between classes. The Negroes migrating to the north, it was felt, would also be welcomed into the new society on a social parity with the whites.

[1] Message to Congress, 1861.

Several developments intervened, however, to halt this trend. First were the decisions of the Supreme Court after the Civil War which countenanced segregation in public places. Then, with advancing industrialization after 1890 came a marked sharpening in the lines between one income group and another. More than ever before, people became identified by economic status and by social position. Discrimination, whether social, religious, or racial, has epidemic qualities. Afflicting one class, it soon spreads to afflict others. It was only a question of time before race and even religion would take their place among the new social classifications of Amerian neighborhoods and the involuntary ghetto replace the voluntary one and become part of America's landscape.

Extensive migrations of ethnic minorities—at first Orientals to the west coast and then Negroes to the cities of the industrial north—began to sharpen class differences. These people came to improve their lot. They undertook the menial tasks which a growing country required. Unfamiliar with our customs or language, they herded together with their own kind. One of their misfortunes was that they came and settled *en masse* and thereby threatened the old pattern of neighborhoods. They competed for shelter and doubled up in the limited dwellings so that they might be able to pay the high rents. They sparked class consciousness on the part of the existing residents. With the further growth of capitalism and the increasing competition for jobs, other emotions were stirred that further sharpened the distinctions between man and man.

With the automobile, new suburbs on the outskirts of cities grew up. They were composed of chaste little villas, paid for with a token down-payment and a life-term mortgage and were bought largely by little people—families earning $2000 to $4000 per annum. Most of them were skilled or clerical workers, small merchants, and folk representing America's great middle class. Thanks partly to propaganda, owning one's home which is a deep-seated emotion in America, had become also a badge of prestige and an honorific value. The excessive mortgage and the insecurity of the tenure meant less to these people than the white door, the quaint blue shutters, the brass knocker, the blue half-tiled bathroom, all of which came to have a sumptuous elegance all its own.

This group also became a ripe field for the speculative builder, the rumor-monger, and the hate-hawker. The common thread that held this group's interests together became "neighborhood dignity." It was not physical blight that came to be feared but intrusion by the "wrong people." And who were the wrong people? The various minorities for whom the private builder had ceased to provide homes.

Subdividers and speculative landlords sensed the new attitudes and conformed to them. They translated prejudice into profits and became less willing to rent or sell to the unwanted minorities. Mortgage-lenders responded to these attitudes, too, and soon rated Negro-occupied property as risky. Welcome as a servant in the house itself, the Negro was now looked upon as an intolerable neighbor. As regional prejudices matured in the west and southwest against Chinese, Japanese, Mexican-Americans, American Indians, and others, restrictive practices embraced more and more minorities and spread throughout the land with increasing contagion.

There grew up the "absolutely restricted neighborhood"

(no Negroes, Jews, or other minorities), and the "reasonably restricted neighborhood" (Jews accepted, but no Negroes). The more races excluded, it was felt, the more "exclusive" the section. The un-American pattern of restricted neighborhoods became a mark of social distinction. The worker who may have had no prejudice against a co-worker who was a Negro became prejudiced against him as a neighbor. In the end, housing became the wedge that split class from class. The American neighborhood became the great breeding ground of racial and color prejudice and discrimination.

A fundamental social change thus arrived in America, unanalyzed and almost unnoticed. Segregation of minorities, once (outside of a few southern states) the voluntary product of economic disadvantages, is now being imposed upon the minorities by duress. Advance in economic status no longer confers freedom to move to better housing. American slums are no longer attributable solely to the gap between rent and family income. Slums for members of minority groups are being created and perpetuated by social biases and pressures. Even those free of any personal prejudice feel impelled to conform to what has now become part of the unwritten code of social ethics.[1]

The methods for keeping minorities in their place were not always confined to the snub or the restrictive covenant. In-migrating Negroes and Chinese have been threatened. Wooden crosses were burned in their front yards. Their children were assaulted on the way to school. How-

---

[1] The United Nations itself, having contracted with the Metropolitan Life Insurance Company in 1947 for several hundred apartments in Stuyvesant Town for its personnel, agreed to let this company screen the applicants on the basis of race and color. Only a disclosure in the *New York Post* and a timely protest by the personnel forced the UN officials to cancel the whole contract.

ever primitive such brutality may have been as a solution
for racial conflict, its lack of legal sanction at least left
room for law, reason, and educational processes to function. The government was not party to it and was free to
intercede. In recent years, however, the discriminatory attitudes of the marketplace were embraced by the government itself. Bias which had been personal, localized, and
often transitory, became institutionalized, widespread,
and lasting. The third and most ominous phase of the
problem was now reached.

4

In 1935, the Federal Housing Administration (FHA)
moved forward to become the main bulwark of the racial
restrictive covenant. By insuring or refusing to insure
mortgages in an area, its administrators became the senti-
nels of racial purity of the American neighborhood and the
palatins of a new American caste system.

"If a neighborhood is to retain stability," said the FHA
Manual, "it is necessary that properties continue to be occupied by the same social and racial classes." The Manual
cautioned its agents to favor "prevention of infiltration";
warned against "adverse influences" which included "un-
harmonious racial groups." The stability of housing communities, it said, depends on occupancy by "the same social and racial classes to which they are accustomed." [1]

Fortified by written sanction, FHA field agents not only

---

[1] Federal Housing Administration: *Underwriting Manual;* 1938.

kept whites, blacks, reds, and yellows in their places, but taught private developers how to do it themselves. Incredible though it may sound, the FHA framed the very restrictive covenants which developers could and did use. All they had to do was to copy the Federal form and fill in the race or religion to be banned.

The Civil Rights Act of 1866 that Negro citizens have the same right as is enjoyed by white citizens to "inherit, purchase, lease, sell, hold, and convey real and personal property" had been nullified by administrative edict of a government agency.

When, in 1946, protest finally matured, this FHA policy had become so entrenched that it could not easily be dislodged. An error once rooted in custom develops a momentum of its own. The perplexed FHA officials simply could not comprehend how they could be expected to abide by the law of the land and the law of the marketplace at the same time. Civil service employees and administrators in America have never been trained in the finer complexities of constitutional ethics. The mores of the suburbs in which they live are the mores they take with them to their desks. Thus, when continued protest finally forced the FHA administrators to modify their sordid little Manual, the rise into the free democratic atmosphere had to be gradual in order to avoid a bad case of administrative bends. And gradual indeed it was.

The first step was taken in 1947 when the revised FHA Manual used more cryptic language: "If a mixture of *user groups* is found to exist it must be determined whether the mixture will render the neighborhood *less desirable to present and prospective occupants. Protective* covenants are essential to the sound development of proposed residential areas since they regulate the use of the land and provide a basis for the development of harmonious, attractive neighborhoods suitable and desirable to the user groups forming the potential market." [1] (Emphasis supplied).

As late as November 19, 1948, Assistant FHA Commissioner W. J. Lockwood was still writing [2] that FHA "has never insured a housing project of mixed occupancy," and then ventured that "we believe that such projects would probably in a short period of time become all-Negro or all-white."

The anti-racial attitude was not confined to FHA alone. A 1944 report on "Neighborhood Conservation" by two consultants to the National Housing Administration deplored the movement "of certain clannish, gregarious foreign-born groups, of religious groups, of social groups, and most important of all, of the great contained and semi-contained groups of Negroes and Jews. We were taught to say in our college economics that 'Bad money drives out good,'" says the report. It then recommends a "drive for restrictive covenants." The report never became official but it was soberly classified as a "first approach" by the Federal director of urban redevelopment.

In 1948, thanks largely to President Truman's leadership, the general atmosphere had become more kindly to civil rights. The basic principles of American social doctrine were reaffirmed in a special government report. [3]

---

[1] Federal Housing Administration, *Underwriting Manual,* January 1947.

[2] To James Cassels, Executive Secretary, National Cooperative Mutual Housing Association, Chicago, Illinois.

[3] President's Committee on Civil Rights, *To Secure These Rights,* Washington, 1947.

In the new atmosphere, the Supreme Court of the United States ruled that, while racial covenants were valid between the parties, judges as agents of the state may not enforce them. The ruling resulted in opening up a few forbidden areas to minorities, but by and large the victory was in theory more than in fact. Legal interpretations and traditional practices carried over many of the old discriminations. A Missouri court in 1949 held that violators of such covenants were answerable in damages to the persons aggrieved. Yet an advance had been made in principle and the way paved for educational processes to operate.

Continued protest against FHA's support of restrictive practices finally resulted in forcing FHA to make public announcement that after February 15, 1950 it would no longer insure mortgages on property subject to racial covenants. The press hailed the announcement as an epochal advance in racial equality, while realtors from coast to coast lamented it as an unconscionable invasion of private prerogatives.

After all this fanfare and breast-beating, a fair appraisal of the result was that the vast amount of property already subject to racial covenants was not affected. The new policy in fact served only to warn the speculative builders who had not already filed covenants of their rights to do so, and it gave them a convenient respite within which to file. While progress was being made at the executive and judicial levels, the fact remained that segregation in housing continued the pattern of American life generally. There is still at this writing not a single mixed FHA rental project. The traditional gap between principle and practice in racial freedom in housing remains almost as wide as ever.

5

Urban redevelopment, the biggest thing since the advent of the gas range, can be either a blessing or a menace. As currently planned, it is a far-reaching usurpation of public prerogatives. The new program borrows its name from private enterprise, but the power and the greenbacks come from the government, Federal and local. Under the Housing Act of 1949, cities may condemn land and resell it to private redevelopment companies at bargain prices; they may also dispossess existing tenants, use Federal and local subsidies, and surrender streets to make the private projects attractive. Once built, the projects are *privately* owned and free of regulation. Though use of the written restrictive covenant is banned, there is nothing in the Federal law or regulations to prevent developers from barring Negro, Catholic, Chinese, or Jewish tenants as they please.

This formula has serious political and social implications. It is a democratic concept that government must be color-blind, creed-blind, and race-blind. There are no first- and second-class citizenships in a democratic society. A democratic government cannot throw slum-dwellers into the streets so that their homesites can be rebuilt with apartments for their betters. That, however, is exactly what can happen under the redevelopment law, and it undoubtedly will happen in many cities, unless the government acts.

Government functions through its powers to tax, to condemn property, and to police. How these powers are exercised spells the difference between free and despotic government. In this democracy, the Bill of Rights is designed to guarantee that public powers will not be used to favor one class against another.

The private entrepreneur, however, has a conscience that is more free from ethical restraints than the government's. In our free enterprise society the entrepreneur is devoted to profit and it is unreasonable to expect him to act like an altruist or conform to the Fourteenth Amendment in his private conduct. He hires as he pleases, rents or sells to whomever he pleases. He has no responsibility for setting an example to the community or for doing what is good. His function is to make money. This in the end is supposed to be good for everybody. The concept runs back to Mandeville's *The Fable of the Bees* (1705) when it was shown that private vices make public virtues, i.e., people working selfishly in their own interests will unconsciously co-operate in working toward the general public good. Adam Smith extended the theory from honey to money in his *Wealth of Nations*.

The concept in this industrial age is a long way from either Mandeville, Smith, or Thomas Jefferson. Still, the profit motive in a free enterprise economy, whatever its inequities, is generally supposed to assure reasonable equality of opportunity. The color of the customer is less decisive than the color of his money. His talent is more influential than his race. In a free market the saleability of goods is influenced more by trade-mark and value than by creed or ancestry. Since this theory does not always stand up in practice, it may become the function of a democratic government to intervene whenever a gang-up on minorities threatens their livelihood, their food, or their shelter.

Thus, hotels and restaurants are often forbidden to discriminate in the selection of guests. Employers are barred from discriminating in carrying out public contracts and sometimes even in private employment. Unions may be kept in line when they enjoy government aid or power. The free-market system, checked by government in its excesses, has indeed produced the system most conducive to racial and social equality the world has ever known.

Yet though private entrepreneurs may claim freedom from government interference when they invest their own money, one thing should be clear—when an undertaking is made possible by government power or funds, it cannot be judged by the same standards as the market place. It must conform to constitutional not private ethics. The urban redevelopment subsidy and power-grant does not come from private enterprise. It is government money and the use of government prerogatives, and the government cannot dispense funds and powers except for the *general* welfare, which means the welfare of all, not some.

When government acts in liaison with private speculators to encourage bias, it becomes the public policy; prejudice then becomes established as the law and policy of the land. Government is no longer the guardian of rights but the instrument of bigotry. That is why urban redevelopment provides an ominous vehicle for constitutional subversion.

Urban redevelopment and any other social reform must be brought under the fold of the constitution or be aban-

doned. This is the challenge that faces the housing pro-
gram today.

6

Segregated housing has been proved wrong not only in theory but also in practice. Throughout the country there are public housing projects where whites and Negroes and other races live together in complete harmony. In many southern cities Negroes and whites live next door to each other in the fluid boundary zones between white and Negro districts. Time has shown that race riots are not started by next-door neighbors. One doesn't lynch the woman from whom one borrows coffee when the stores are closed.

Public housing projects in New York City, Philadelphia, New Haven, Los Angeles, Chicago, Pittsburgh, and Seattle—to name some of the cities—have proved that whites and blacks can get along just as well as whites and whites or blacks and blacks. These mixed housing projects have had little or no attention in newspapers and magazines. For some years the local housing authorities were reluctant to publicize the success of their ventures, possibly through fear of what southern Congressmen would say about this use of a Federal subsidy. Yet such projects may mark the most important gain in the struggle for racial equality since the Civil War.

These mixed housing projects have not been uniform in pattern. Some housing authorities have deliberately and timidly assigned Negroes and whites to separate buildings in the same project. Others admitted only a few token families of Negroes. Many, however, have literally ignored the color line, with the result that Negroes comprise a substantial percentage of the tenants.

The most successful projects have been those where the Negro tenants were part of an interracial community and were sufficiently represented so they could enjoy the self-security that an ostracized race requires for its comfort in a new environment. In these projects initial tensions have disappeared, differences have been adjusted, a peaceful atmosphere has been created.

In contrast, there has been much less accomplished in projects where the minority receives only token representation or where the races have been separated by buildings or some other line of demarcation. There is no way to separate without separating. Any method used tends to emphasize the distinctions and reinforce the old prejudices. Tenants in these projects cling to the attitudes common in private developments. White and Negro children may attend the same public school, even go to the same summer camp—but when they are back on segregated ground the white children do not play with Negro youngsters.

The picture is just the opposite in projects that are completely mixed. Children play together with no consciousness of color. Tenant associations hold business meetings and give parties. Neighbors visit back and forth. *If only two or three such projects had proved successful, the story would have been significant news. The fact is that every properly administered project has succeeded.*

"There has been no tendency for neighborhood people to move away because of the projects," said General Thomas F. Farrell, chairman of the New York City Housing Authority. "The projects are well built and well maintained. Business in the neighborhood improves. With rare exceptions the tenants are good neighbors." [1] The impressive number of similar experiences shows that inter-racial living is now more than an experiment. It is a signal demonstration of a workable way of life, a possible key to America's Number One problem.

The feeling of white superiority seems to subside and then disappear when people live together as neighbors and share the common responsibilities for its success. Project managers have overcome the initial objection of some of the white tenants by explaining the policies of the authority and there have been very few instances of tenants moving out even where comparable dwellings in other projects were offered them. The common use of recreational facilities has been an important factor in creating the environment for an accord. The Negroes are members of the tenant associations, participate in the cultural programs, often lead in the community activities.

There have been problems. Not all have responded as have some. But the problems have not been a fraction of what was predicted nor have they been serious. *The evils of segregation do not arise from either whites or Negroes. They come from segregation. When that barrier is removed, the whites and Negroes get along without trouble.*

---

[1] Thomas F. Farrell: "Object Lesson in Race Relations," *The New York Times Magazine*, February 12, 1950, p. 37. See also Robert P. Weaver: *The Negro Ghetto* (New York: Harcourt, Brace and Company; 1948) and Charles Abrams: *Race Bias in Housing* (New York: American Civil Liberties Union; 1946).

7

The success of inter-racial public housing has already had a tonic effect on large-scale private housing. The traditional fear of private investors has been that the entry of one Negro family into a white neighborhood will signal a mass infiltration. Infiltration is supposed to mean loss of social status, depreciation of the neighborhood, and a sharp decline in property values. Hence the restrictive covenant, to protect the white majority against potential invasion by the house-hungry Negro.

When building sites consisted of small lots, with no large-scale planning for an area, the pattern of segregation could hardly be changed. The infiltration of one or a few minority families into an "established" neighborhood meant the fear of an inundation by the minority group. The result was the panic sale of properties and the removal of the old tenantry. But the new approach to housing is the community of substantial size that creates its own environment. Here lies the opportunity in public housing and the FHA program, in urban redevelopment, and in co-operative housing.

Private investors in large mixed projects are discovering that the presence of Negroes or other minorities will not affect their investments. There is no change in the social status of the tenants or the character of the neighborhood. When a New York City ordinance in 1944 barred discrimination in tax-exempt projects, critics predicted that no more such private projects would be launched. Higher income families, it was said, would not live in mixed projects and private investors and mortgage lenders would refuse to risk their money. Pressure for repeal of the ordinance was unremitting.

The critics were wrong. Millions in private funds have been invested in projects subject to the ordinance. The Mutual Life Insurance Company agreed in October 1948 to an 80% loan on the Queensview project in Queens, which has more than 25 non-white families among its 731 unbiased co-operators. The co-operators are families with incomes up to $6,990 who make a down payment of $600 per room. At the first meeting of the co-operators, one member asked whether Negroes would be admitted. The chairman said they would and braced himself for a wholesale withdrawal of applications. There was spontaneous applause from the tenants. Only one family pulled out.

The Amalgamated Houses are co-operative undertakings financed by the Bowery Savings Bank and the Mutual Life Insurance Company for 1,550 tenants. Three Negro families have purchased apartments in Hillman Houses, its lower east side development. The United Nations non-tax-exempt project in Queens, located in a white area, has operated since its inception as a mixed undertaking, housing people of all races and colors. The new non-subsidized or self-supporting $300 million New York City program is non-segregated and the Negro minority will be substantially represented. When the first project in this program was announced, 30,000 applications were made in a single day. In private as well as in public housing the initial barrier has been broken in New York City.[1] Even Metropoli-

---

[1] Henry Bruere, explaining the reasons for investment by his bank,

tan Life Insurance Company's $93 million Stuyvesant Town project has now yielded to the experience and has accepted Negro tenants.

Although inter-racial private housing is still in the development stage, the success of inter-racial public housing during the past decade is the final answer to the sceptics who have said that the races cannot be mixed without causing trouble. What really causes trouble, as the sociologists have observed, is segregation and its by-products: guilt feelings and fear on the part of the dominant whites, resentment and hatred by the injured minority, unstable neighborhoods, tensions.

It is significant that while New York City was forging ahead with private redevelopments under its non-discrimination ordinance, there was not a single private project undertaken in other states or in upstate New York—where discrimination *could* be freely practiced. One reason may be that financial institutions are more ready to invest where the issue is settled, but will hesitate to accept public aid for a discriminatory project when there is a good chance of a legal fight or public hostility. Public opinion may tolerate discrimination in wholly private undertakings but when public money is involved, fair play becomes the issue. Few institutions are willing to face the recriminations that were heaped on the Metropolitan Life Insurance Company when it first barred Negroes from Stuyvesant Town.

The Bowery Savings Bank, in non-discriminatory private projects to the extent of $13.5 million, says he considers the loans "sagacious." He informed the writer that "our approach is pragmatic and not governed by prejudice or unawareness of new social habits."

8

The current government housing program presents a
serious threat to democratic principles and also a magnifi-
cent opportunity. The program can be either an opening
wedge to the dissolution of enforced segregation or the
destruction of any hope for inter-racial understanding and
harmony. There is no such state as "separate but equal."
Men who are separate can never have equal opportunity.

Federal and local officials must not become the pawns
of private bigotry. They must see the opportunity they
have in their grasp, envision themselves as trustees of a
higher code than that of the huckster—they are the guard-
ians of constitutional principles.

The claim is made that the southern states will object.
This has been the stock answer. It has served as a convenient buffer for weakling officials in northern areas, many of
whom are cementing segregation today.[1]

The southern states constitute, indeed, a special prob-

---

[1] " 'No large city is doing more than C—— to keep the Negro in
segregated neighborhoods. In the past decade, the Negro population has
soared past 400,000, an increase of close to 45 per cent as against 6 per
cent for whites. New arrivals have been wedged into the old slums . . .
Public housing is solidly Jim Crow in D——. Negroes whose housing
need is most acute have been allotted a smaller proportion of dwellings
. . . A trifling spark could touch off wholesale murder.'—Public Affairs
Committee pamphlet on housing.

"The cities referred to are not Chattanooga and Dallas. They are
Chicago and Detroit, where citizens view with horror the backwardness
of the benighted South." An editorial in the *New York Post*, April 23,
1951.

lem and a difficult one. There, neighborhood segregation is often less than in the north, though social segregation and segregation in facilities is the rule. But social segregation is only one phase of the deeper problem of overall segregation that must be tackled. The question is one of timing. In the south, the first steps should be to reinforce the Negro's political rights, to win him the right to vote, to grant him equality in education and employment. Meanwhile, every effort should be made to preserve whatever mixed neighborhood patterns prevail in many southern cities and there should be no retreat from gains already made. *Elimination of the housing shortage is the first prerequisite to better inter-racial understanding in the south.*

Timing and strategy are as vital in the fight for equality as the statement of principles. The housing effort to which the south has given co-operation is a sound strategic step in the long fight for social and political equality.

In the north, however, segregation was not always the accepted practice. The minorities lived as part of the mixed community. Today, in many cities, segregation is bringing about new permanent patterns of segregation in schools, playgrounds, and shopping centers. The southern ideology should not become the common denominator for the nation or the pretext for segregation where segregation has never before existed.

9

These are the specific immediate advances to be sought:

1. Progressive opinion should be mobilized to ease the housing shortage for lower and middle-income groups. If people of all races are provided with decent housing there will be no fear of mass shifts in the racial composition of neighborhoods, and the first cause for segregation would thereby be removed.

2. The successful formula of inter-racial occupancy adopted by the many local housing agencies should be continued and expanded. Information on the successful experience of inter-racial occupancy should be disseminated for the guidance of all local authorities. The aim should be the extension of such policies. The government agencies concerned with housing have the responsibility for this.

3. Slum clearance and urban redevelopment projects should be postponed and new homes should be built on vacant land until the housing shortage has ended and until satisfactory evidence is adduced that suitable dwellings at the same rents are available to tenants or buildings to be demolished.

4. The creation by public and private enterprise of new neighborhoods with self-contained environments should be promoted as the most effective means of furthering understanding between races and breaking down segregation.

5. In all urban redevelopment projects where public aid or power is used, minorities should be granted equal right to live in the new dwellings.

6. The Federal Housing Administration should be barred from lending its aid to developers who promote restricted neighborhoods. While discriminatory practices of this government agency have been modified for the better, a wide gap between its field policies and the constitution still exists. This should be bridged by effective presidential action.

7. Mixed housing should be treated as an infant industry deserving of encouragement by government through subsidies, demonstration projects, and loans until it becomes accepted by communities and investors.

8. A permanent commission on civil and political rights should be set up by the President, whose tasks should include the continuous education of the public in the principles and practice of equality. It should guide Federal housing agencies in moving continually forward toward elimination of all discrimination in housing in America.

America is faced with a choice. It can continue to countenance the pattern of racial segregation, exclude proscribed groups, incite racial tensions, continue to acquiesce in a scheme of living that is a challenge not only to real estate stability but to common-sense democracy. Or, it can at long last try to break through the barriers that have stood in the way of racial harmony and understanding. The choice may seem hard and the program difficult to achieve, but the public housing experiment has demonstrated that it can be done. A world is involved in the principle.

XIII. *The Role of the States*

BY

Chester Bowles

[Chester Bowles, U. S. Ambassador to India and Nepal, has been a leading figure in government and private business enterprise for more than a decade. As Administrator of the Office of Price Administration (OPA) during World War II, his was the achievement of maintaining a relatively stable price structure throughout the war years.

[In 1948, Chester Bowles was elected governor of the State of Connecticut. Shortly thereafter, he inaugurated a plan for bringing down the cost of housing for middle-income families. The plan is unlike anything attempted before, either in this country or abroad. It is described in this chapter.]

1

SHOULD our state governments assume any responsibility for public housing?

So far, with the exception of only ten states, the whole responsibility and initiative on public housing has been left to Federal, city, and county governments. By and large it is Federal-municipal—not state—programs which are clearing our slums, building low-cost homes, stimulating private construction and tackling the thorny problem of middle-income housing.

I am convinced, however, that housing is one of the important areas where the states not only can but should take aggressive and positive action.

The part the Federal government must always play in public housing is, of course, very great. In slum clearance, in redevelopment, in housing research, in mortgage loan programs to home builders and buyers, the Federal government provides assistance of a size, kind, and quality no state government can afford to duplicate.

But our Connecticut experience has proved to me very emphatically that a state government can initiate and carry through an effective housing program that is both a necessary and valuable supplement to Federal and local programs.

It can, for instance, provide excellent moderate income housing, for shelter rents as low as $37 a month, for two-bedroom units, and without cost to the taxpayers. It can test, on a small scale, new types of housing programs and financing methods that would be impractical for the Federal government to attempt. It can co-ordinate the activities and raise the standards of performance of local housing authorities in direct day-to-day contacts impossible for a distant Federal government. And it can encourage further slum clearance, redevelopment, and low-rent housing, both by providing funds to supplement Federal grants, and by providing the local on-the-spot stimulus to action so often needed.

The question is an even larger one that this. It has a very important bearing on our whole concept of democratic government, and the relation of state and Federal powers. To ask the Federal government, plus a few city governments, to carry the whole load on housing—or any major public service—is to overlook what should be one of the most important roles of state governments. It invites what I believe to be increased and unhealthy dependence on the Federal government in a field where the states can and should carry their own share of the responsibility.

After listening for over two years to stormy legislative and political debate on housing in Connecticut, I have no illusions that a state housing program is all clear sailing. Opponents to public housing rise up in state capitols and state political parties—as they do in Washington.

But as I have watched the first 6000 families move into clean, decent homes renting for only $37 to $45 a month, I can only say, with feeling, that the service a state housing program can provide is well worth a few political and legislative headaches.

2

The American people have become firmly convinced that good housing is a fundamental human right in a democracy. They have increasingly shown that, wherever good housing cannot be financed through usual or private means, the job of developing other means is a responsibility of their government.

Our Federal government has customarily shared the financial and administrative responsibility for such programs directly with local governments.

This partnership developed naturally. Housing has only become recognized as a government responsibility in the last twenty years, and in the depths of the deep depression few of our states were financially able to launch new government services. The Federal government with its far greater credit resources was left to take the entire initiative.

These early Federal housing and slum clearance programs were designed to increase employment and stimulate recovery in the all-important field of construction, as well as to provide better housing for low-income families. Since both needs were urgent and pressing, the Federal program established direct working relationships with the cities, without waiting for the more cumbersome state governments slowly to recognize their responsibilities. It was not until 1938 that New York State, the first state to take action, set up its own comprehensive state program for low-rent housing.

Fortunately more and more states have now begun to realize that they, too, have very strong reasons to move into active creative partnership with the Federal and city governments. In large part, this realization has come about since World War II, when the urgent need for veterans' homes so acutely dramatized America's basic housing shortage.

Connecticut's housing situation after the War was typical of industrial states throughout the nation. Largely because of the heavy influx of war workers to Connecticut's many specialized war industries, we have had a population increase of about 300,000 in the past ten years. With the exception of 5000 temporary shelters for war workers, provided by the Federal government, there was virtually no home building during World War II. According to the best available figures, we, a small state of only two million people, found ourselves in 1946 with a shortage of between 70,000 and 100,000 homes. Some 37,000 families were living doubled up with relatives and friends, and another 42,000 were living in substandard homes—in other words, in slums.

Private enterprise was willing and able to finance only about 7000 to 8000 homes a year. And after the elimination of the Federal Veteran's Emergency Housing Program in 1946, these homes were being built only for the high-income brackets, mostly at sale prices of $15,000 and up, and at rents of $90 a month and up.

By 1945 veterans groups throughout Connecticut began an indignant series of appeals to their state legislature. There was no question in their minds, at least, that their state government had the responsibility for providing homes, although such state responsibility was entirely without precedent in Connecticut, as practically everywhere else.

In 1947, the Connecticut legislature reluctantly agreed to take limited action. It authorized the State Housing Authority to guarantee the interest and principal on $15 million worth of bonds issued by local housing authorities. With these bonds, it was assumed that the local authorities could build roughly 1500 homes, for shelter rents of $55 to $60 for two-bedroom units.

In short, Connecticut, in its very first venture into public housing, chose the almost unexplored and highly con-

troversial moderate-rental field. The state legislature did this for two principal reasons: first, it wished to meet the veteran's demands without spending any money—and, therefore, chose a virtually self-liquidating moderate-rent program; second, it expected that the Federal government would soon launch a new subsidized low-rent program.

A year later, when not one of the promised homes had yet been built, Connecticut's veterans threatened a mass encampment on our capitol grounds. As a result, a special legislative session, in August 1948, voted an additional $30 million for moderate rental housing, at the same $55 to $60 per month.

The demand for speedy, effective action in cutting out the delays and red tape, and actually getting their homes built, together with a major expansion of the program itself, became a principle issue in my campaign for governor that same fall.

3

Immediately upon my inaugural I asked for the legislative authorization for a $100 million state bond issue to build 10,000 additional homes. We expected that 5000 of these homes would rent at $50 to $55 a month; the second 5000 through the use of subsidies would rent from $20 to $45. We also asked that the 3000 homes which had been authorized in the special session be placed on the same 50–50 subsidized basis. This total of 13,000 homes was almost double the number of homes built and financed by private enterprise in the biggest previous building year.

The ensuing battle on this proposal was hard fought and sometimes bitter. But I believe that some of the problems that it raised, together with the solutions finally agreed to, may be both interesting and instructive to anyone attempting a state program.

Our state legislature, like many throughout America, has been virtually controlled by a House of Representatives whose members come largely from small towns and rural areas. Indifference or even hostility to the needs of city dwellers—of which housing is one—is traditional. Democrats, who strongly favored public housing, were outnumbered 2 to 1 by the Republicans who opposed it, and who have maintained a firm grip on the Connecticut House for nearly 100 years.

From Connecticut's small town and rural group in the legislature strong opposition arose, not unexpectedly, to our subsidy proposal. Subsidies were, it appeared, socialistic, if not communistic, and would clearly bankrupt the state—the same too familiar arguments.

A second unexpected point of opposition, from in and out of the legislature, and from people of various political persuasions, was that our proposal offered no provision for home ownership, and would thus eventually turn the bulk of our veterans into renters.

I therefore submitted a second proposal to meet these objections. I dropped with very real reluctance the original proposals providing subsidized housing for low-income families. To offset this loss, I suggested a plan whereby rents could be lowered to an average shelter rent of $32 a month. This plan, which I believe represents a new approach to the problem of lower rentals, was as follows:

1. The state would finance approved local housing authority projects with one-year state notes at an anticipated average interest rate of 0.8% instead of the usual 50-year bonds with an interest rate of 2.6%. These notes were to be re-negotiated every year.
2. The state would pay the municipality up to 10% of shelter rent in lieu of taxes.
3. The state would pay a sufficiently high proportion of the interest rate on the bonds to enable local housing authorities to maintain average shelter rents of about $32 monthly.

This program had one serious disadvantage in that it would not provide the very low rentals necessary which many thousands of our low-income families required. But $32 was still a low rent and the total cost of this program to the state, for 13,000 homes, would come to only about $500,000 annually—one-third of the cost originally proposed.

To meet the second objection—the lack of a home ownership provision—I suggested that renters could buy their homes over a period of years by applying a portion of their rental payments to the purchase price.

The House of Representatives flatly refused to accept even the limited subsidy plan of points 2 and 3. They agreed, however, to the critical and key point of the proposal: direct, short term, low-cost financing by the state. This provision would bring shelter rents down to an average of $41 a month, $9 more than the compromise plan, but still far less than any previous proposals, and without cost of any kind to the taxpayers. All administration costs, both state and local, were included in the rents. Overall

income limits were set at six times the shelter rent, plus
$300 for each dependent.

Another $60 million (also to be provided by issuance of
one year notes) was authorized for a home ownership program. As far as we can determine, this part of Connecticut's housing program also established a precedent.

4

Under this unique plan, families of moderate income
($2500, plus $600 for each dependent) who wished to buy
a house, and who could not otherwise meet usual financing charges, may borrow from the state to buy a newly
built house at 1½% interest. With this state aid, families
could purchase homes at monthly payments about $12 to
$16 below normal home financing costs.

For example, a $10,000 home financed under the cus-
tomary FHA plan, with a 25-year mortgage bearing 4¼%
interest, requires a monthly payment of $47.16. The same
$10,000 house can be financed under our Connecticut plan
with a payment for amortization and interest of only
$34.79,[1] a saving of $12.37 a month.

This home-ownership plan was also to be completely
self-supporting, with all administrative, interest and other
costs paid back by the purchasing families as part of each

---

[1] Payments quoted for the FHA house and for the house under the
Connecticut plan provide only for interest and amortization of the $8700
mortgage and do not include taxes, insurance, repairs, upkeep, or utilities.

monthly payment. Under this unique program, over 6000 homes are now occupied.

Specifically this is how this program works: the head of a family first applies to the State Housing Authority for certification of eligibility on the basis of income and housing need. If he is granted a certificate, he chooses an FHA or VA approved house, already built by an operative builder, or to be built by the family's own contractor, or even by his own labor. Next, the family goes to a state authorized private loan correspondent, usually a local bank which has been approved by the state authority, to apply for an FHA or VA loan.

	VETERAN	NON-VETERAN
PRICE OF PROPERTY	$8,000	$8,000
FHA or VA valuation	8,000	8,000
FHA mortgage (Sec. 203)	—	7,100
VA (2nd) mortgage (Sec. 501)	8,000	
CASH REQUIRED		
Balance of price	$ —	$ 900
Other settlement costs	80	71
Prepaid items	89	124
	$ 169	$1,095
MONTHLY EXPENSE		
State FHA loan, 25 yrs., 1½%	—	$ 28.40
State GI loan, 30 yrs., 1½%	$ 27.61	—
FHA mortgage insurance premium	—	2.86
Taxes (¹⁄₁₂ of annual taxes)	8.50	8.50
Insurance	1.35	1.35
TOTAL FINANCING COSTS	$ 37.46	$41.11

If accepted, the family gets a state mortgage loan to buy or build the house at 1½% interest. The operative builder is eligible for construction loans at 3% from the state. At a cost of $50 a house, he can also take out insurance against his failure to sell any homes which have been approved by the state for at least 90% of the established value.

The foregoing table shows typical financing charges for an $8000 house. The monthly expense covers financing only. It does not include insurance, light, heat, water, repairs, replacements, and other incidental expenses of home ownership.

The vital point in the program is the 1½% interest rate, which saves the family $10 to $14 a month. To those accustomed to mortgage rates of 4½% or more, this may look like a subsidy. It is not. The home-ownership plan is completely self-supporting. Administrative, interest, and other costs are fully paid by the family out of the 1½% rate. Here is how:

Expected average rate of interest	.8%
Hedge against higher rate	.1%
Administrative costs	.1%
Fees to banks and loan correspondents	
processing loans	.5%
	1.50%

The plan depends, of course, on short term borrowing by the state at a low interest rate.

To get the utmost co-operation from private builders, state-wide and city-wide meetings were called. The program was carefully explained to builders, realtors, materials suppliers, and their trade associations. Except for a few bitter enders, it was accepted with enthusiasm.

Our special concern was to build as many houses as possible for less than $9,000. Demand is greatest for houses priced at about $8,000. Despite earnest efforts by the builders, we were not able to produce as many dwellings as we had hoped for in the $8,000 price class. The average price was around $8,900.

One reason for the excellent co-operation from private enterprise was our decision to work through private banks and lending institutions instead of setting up a separate agency to process the loans. Technical regulations were formulated with the advice of the banks and other private loan correspondents who, as with the FHA program, get one-half of 1% of the total amount of the loan outstanding.

Some lenders and builders were at first fearful that our program would compete with private and FHA financing. Analysis showed this would not happen. The state program was designed for families who could not get mortgage help elsewhere; at the very most the overlap was estimated at only 5%. In short, the state was opening an entirely new market for home buying.

At the request of the builders, the state housing authority analyzed the market to determine in what areas there was greatest demand for houses, and at what price levels. The analysis, which was based upon applications for state loans, was the first of its kind in Connecticut and has proved extremely valuable to the building industry and to lending agencies.

As a guide to interested families the state also made a careful survey of builders' plans, showing how many homes the builders in various cities were planning to put up, what types, and at what prices.

Housing experts expressed special interest in our short-term loans for financing both the home-ownership and moderate rental programs. The average interest rate has been less than 0.9%. Since the notes must be re-issued each year, what about the possibility of much higher rates which would compel us to increase rents and mortgage payments?

Our system gives protection against fluctuations because both the local housing authorities and the individual home buyers pay slightly more than the actual present cost of the loan. The sums accumulated by these charges constitute a reserve against a rise in interest rates.

5

In summary, Connecticut's housing program, both rental and home ownership, is providing more than 12,000 dwellings for middle-income families without cost to the taxpayers. The program does not, as I pointed out earlier, provide low-rent housing for families at the bottom of the wage scale. The Connecticut legislature left that job entirely to the Federal government. I feel strongly, however, that the state must ultimately share with the Federal government the responsibility for low rent housing.[1]

What Connecticut established is a most desirable kind of shared responsibility between state and local govern-

---

[1] A few states have already accepted this responsibility. Of the ten which have housing programs, seven provide some form of subsidy or capital grant. There is wide variation in the kind of aid given. All that most of the states have done is to pass legislation enabling localities to use Federal aid in the construction and operation of low rent housing.

ments, and between government and private enterprise. It has effectively shown, I believe, that a government housing program is not a threat to private industry, but a tremendous stimulus to private building activity.

Private enterprise handles almost every phase of the state program. Local housing authorities use private architects. They turn over construction to private building contractors who buy the building materials from private sources and employ labor, working under the usual conditions of private business. In the home ownership program, private builders also do all the work. Moreover, all of the financing—including the processing of state mortgage loans—is done through private banks and private lending agencies.

The entire program increased the total number of homes built in Connecticut in 1950 by 100% over previous yearly records—in other words, it has provided homes that simply would not have been built without a state program.

The initiative to build rental units must come directly from the communities through their local housing authorities. In Connecticut there are now forty-three of these local groups. The essential local liaison can be carried on only by a state authority. Familiarity with local problems and personnel, with political over- and under-tones in local communities, intimate knowledge of state legislation affecting site acquisition and land assembly, are indispensable. Being constantly available to local authorities, in frequent touch with them by telephone or personal visit, is not only immensely helpful, but essential. There are also regular monthly meetings with the local authorities at the state capitol.

"Trouble-shooting," at the state level, is also necessary. In one case, for instance, our highway department was holding as a right-of-way a sector of land needed by a local authority, to complete its project. Our state housing authority, with the governor's office, was able to straighten out this tangle and get the long delayed project under way.

In another instance, in New London, the local housing authority ran into trouble on local zoning laws. A so-called "Taxpayers League" (actually they were largely rooming house operators who wished to block public housing) had attempted to block modification of the zoning laws to permit a 144-home project to be built. The state housing authority, exercising its powers for the first time granted in the State Housing Act, waived the zoning restrictions and permitted the New London Housing Authority to start construction. A public referendum subsequently sustained the state action by a 2 to 1 majority.

Our state housing authority reviews local site and architectual plans and construction bids and approves them only if they meet high over-all-agreed-upon standards as to cost, rent level, and construction. Broad leeway is allowed, however, on type of home and architectural style. As a result state housing rental projects are divided between garden type, duplex, and single dwelling units.

The state also maintains on-the-site inspection of all local construction. We feel that this inspection is necessary to protect both the tenants and the state's investment.

A stiff anti-discrimination act, on which we insisted as part of the overall housing program, protects all tenants, prospective tenants, and buyers against discrimination on the grounds of religion, race, creed or color.

A very important function of Connecticut's Authority has been to establish a "speed-up" system that will minimize, if not eliminate, the usual lags and delays at each step of the planning and construction process. Obviously, this is again a task that only a state agency, in constant close touch with the local housing authorities, is in the best position to do. In co-operation with builders and contractors, Connecticut has now set up planning and construction schedules with rigid deadlines to cover each step from the earmarking of funds to final completion and occupancy.

These rigid and realistic deadlines have resulted in a very sharp speed-up in our construction schedules. One project of 80 homes, in East Hartford, was ready for initial occupancy in 200 days, against a previous 345-day period for similar construction.

6

During the acute post-war housing shortage, we all had to devote our immediate efforts to getting roofs over the heads of our veterans and homeless families. But, as I have studied the long-term role of state governments on housing and mapped plans for the future of our own housing authority, it is clear to me that a well-rounded state program must include many other valuable and important housing services.

1. *Redevelopment.* Certainly whatever action the Federal government may take, it is highly important that a

state adopt an urban and regional redevelopment program on a state-wide basis. So far as I know, Illinois and Pennsylvania are the only states which have initiated such a program.

A good redevelopment program should include, in my view, direct supervisory assistance from the state in community planning, land clearance and assembly, and in integrating Federal programs. It should include a state redevelopment law, not only enabling localities to participate in Federal programs but to take any other necessary steps to get local sites cleared and redeveloped.

2. *Clearing House.* Obviously the state should surely act as clearing house and co-ordinating agency for all related construction and development programs of the state, such as highway, park, and school construction, which affect community planning and which need correlation under any long term plans for redevelopment. The state can stimulate better planning and improved architecture by making available to local groups the best experience now being developed throughout the United States. The state should at very least be the stimulus to localities to undertake necessary redevelopment and participate in any Federal programs.

Connecticut has already undertaken some of these functions, though in a limited way. I believe Connecticut might set up a special division on redevelopment, as part of the state housing authority, to extend these activities.

3. *Limited dividend and co-operative housing.* Fourteen states have adopted limited dividend corporation laws to facilitate construction of moderate rental housing. Achievements have not been spectacular and rents are too high, but the method is worth continuing study and trial.

Special attention should be paid to co-operatives, which appear to be one of the most hopeful methods of serving middle-income families. In Connecticut we have been exploring the possibilities of aiding co-operatives through our home-ownership program, again in conjunction with FHA.

4. *Information services.* As an aid to builders and as a guide for state programs, a state housing agency should prepare data on income levels throughout the state. Data on population shifts should also be made available. The state agency is the logical clearing house for all Federal information on housing research, redevelopment, and other Federal activities.

5. *Race relations.* The state housing agency should work with the state interracial commission, if one exists, and with housing authorities and human relations commissions in the communities to prevent discrimination in public housing. Connecticut became in 1949 the first state specifically to prohibit not only discrimination but also segregation in public housing.

6. *School planning.* The state housing authority should work closely with the state department of education to make sure that adequate school facilities are planned for large housing projects. It is my belief and it was my recommendation to the legislature that the state should pay up to 80% of local school building costs when a new school is required to serve a housing project. When this is done, local opposition to new housing projects will often be vigorous because of the fear of tax increases for new school building.

7. *Training Courses.* Few universities and colleges offer training in public housing administration and manage-

ment, yet demand for trained state personnel is very high. The state housing agency should encourage more institutions, especially its state university, to offer such courses.

8. *Employment stabilization.* Maintenance of employment in the critical construction industry is of high importance. Major responsibility for this function should be undertaken, I feel, by the state housing authority. Through official and private sources, a continuous check on the volume of building and employment should be made. As a second phase of this job, the state should seek to co-ordinate all construction by state and Federal agencies. This can best be accomplished by merging the state housing authority into a State Department of Public Works which will greatly facilitate over-all planning.

9. *Building code simplification.* Many building codes are hopelessly outdated and restrictive. There is little chance that each municipality will undertake the expensive and tedious task of revision.

10. *Improvement of standards.* The state housing authority should work with private architects and local housing authorities to encourage high architectural standards not only in public housing but also in private building. Far too many architectural horrors are being tolerated today in the name of moderate cost—and some of the higher priced housing is even less excusable.

11. *Strengthening of the tax structure.* The real estate tax is the mainstay of local government. As governmental services have expanded, the burden on real estate in many cities has come dangerously close to the breaking point. When that point is reached, the municipalities will turn to their state government for rescue. A wise state government should not wait until disaster comes to its door. It should

act in time to head off a crisis by developing a sounder tax structure.

One step would be to help cities and towns clear slums and blighted areas which now drain the local treasury. Outright assistance given early would be cheaper than bailing out bankrupt communities later. Another step would be to encourage municipalities to develop raw land for home building as a new and steadier source of tax revenue.

There are undoubtedly many other housing activities that a progressive state government could profitably undertake. I believe, however, I have sketched in enough of them to indicate the tremendous role that a state government can and should play, if it is willing to accept its mature responsibilities.

I think it should be obvious from this summary that a state government must take an active aggressive part along with the Federal and local governments, if we are to develop a well-rounded housing program for the nation as a whole. In doing so, I feel they will also make a great contribution to democratic government and to the cause of democracy itself.

XIV. *The Rocky Road of Progress*

1

THE ENEMIES of public housing, more noisy than numerous, are heirs to a hundred-year-old tradition. Unable to recruit logic or ethics to their cause, they profess to fear that it is a cloak which conceals an alien philosophy. Such a thing they say, would destroy the American free enterprise system. In short, public housing is socialism.

This fear of "socialistic" low-rent housing generally afflicts only the real estate interests and their spokesmen. There have been few complaints from mayors of cities where public housing has cleared slum areas or from the tenants introduced for the first time to the alien philosophy of the socialistic bathtub.

The core of the opposition to public housing is the National Association of Real Estate Boards. *Their* concept of government has been set forth with admirable clarity by their executive secretary, Herbert U. Nelson: "I do not believe in democracy. I think it stinks. I don't think anybody except direct taxpayers should be allowed to vote. I don't believe women should be allowed to vote at all." [1]

---

[1] The letter containing this statement was written by Mr. Nelson to T. H. Maenner, executive secretary of the NAREB, and was made public during hearings of the House Select Committee on Lobbying Activities on April 19, 1950. See the New York *Daily News,* April 20, 1950.

To impose this philosophy in the field of housing, real estate lobbyists and those who do their bidding in Congress, state legislatures, and city councils, have relied on the time-worn opposition tactics of the last century. They have contributed hardly a single new roadblock on the rocky road which must be traveled by all social progress. Senator Byrd summed it up in the charge that "expansion of socialistic legislation—socialized housing, etc.—if adopted, will destroy the free enterprise system." [1]

Less than seventy years ago, free public education was considered a similar menace. In 1886, Zachariah Montgomery, later an assistant Attorney General, was one of a multitude of good people who railed against "this Communistic system of public schools." [2] Free public education had hardly been accepted as part of the American way, when defenders of sound government and free enterprise undertook to defend the nation against "chimerical" and "foolish" national public highways. [3]

A century ago when courageous women began to demand the right to vote, they were denounced for advocating "unblushing female socialism which defies alike apostles and prophets. In this respect no kindred movement is so decidedly infidel, so rancorously and avowedly anti-biblical." [4]

---

[1] Senator Harry F. Byrd (D., Virginia) in an address before the National Tax Association, quoted in the *Wall Street Journal*, September 14, 1950.

[2] In an article entitled *Poison Drops in the Federal Senate, the School Question from a Parental and Non-Sectarian Stand-Point*.

[3] In 1893 Governor Roswell P. Flower of New York wrote in the *North American Review* that the cost of national highways would be "inconceivable." The task of constructing them "would overwhelm the government" and "the project is too chimerical and foolish to be possible of realization and we might as well dismiss it from serious consideration."

[4] *Harper's New Monthly Magazine*, November 1853.

When the campaign was launched for a child labor amendment to the Constitution, its advocates—in all innocence—proposed that newspaper publishers be counted as employers of children (newsboys). Although passed by Congress in 1924, the amendment is still eight states short of ratification today, largely as a result of press opposition. "The measure is essentially Socialistic, and if ratified will mark the longest step yet proposed for Socializing our Government," said the respected Louisville *Courier-Journal* in 1934.[1] Even the eminent Catholic periodical, *The Commonweal*, abetted the publishers' crusade in an article, asserting that the amendment would enable Congress to "Russianize" American children.[2]

The construction of Hoover Dam opened great areas to irrigation, eliminated the menace of floods, provided abundant electric power, and was a blessing to the southwest. Yet this proposal to dam the Colorado River was characterized in Congress as the "first long stride toward Communism."[3]

American trade unionists in their 150-year fight for freedom to organize were frequently arrested for criminal conspiracy.[4] Later they were vilified as "socialists," "communists," and "anarchists" from the day the words were first discovered by employers.

Leaders of the great railroad strike of 1877 were characterized as "men dominated by the devilish spirit of

---

[1] January 2, 1934. Three years later the *Courier-Journal* reversed its position.

[2] In the issue of April 13, 1934. The article was ably answered on May 25 by Monsignor John A. Ryan.

[3] Representative William H. Sproul (R., Kansas) speaking in the House of Representatives on May 24, 1928.

[4] Foster Rhea Dulles: *Labor in America* (New York: Thomas Y. Crowell; 1949), p. 29.

communism." [1] As late as 1902, some employers still claimed that they had a divine mission to decide the fate of the laborer. George F. Baer, spokesman for the coal operators in the 1902 strike, represented himself as also the spokesman for God. "The rights and interests of the laboring man," he said, "will be protected and cared for not by the labor agitators but by the Christian men to whom God in his infinite wisdom has given the control of the property interests of the country." [2]

2

"Socialism" and "communism" had been virtually exhausted as *theoretical* menaces by the time the Bolsheviks won the Russian civil war. The menace of "communism" could, thereafter, be exploited even more effectively to suit the purposes of reactionaries. Thus, when workers in the steel industry went on strike to improve intolerable conditions, the steel companies announced in full-page ads that Americans would "never stand for the red rule of Bolshevism, IWWism, and any other ism that seeks to tear down the Constitution." [3] Of course, as an investigating commission from the Inter-Church World Movement found, there was not the slightest basis for the charge. But the strikers lost and for twenty years hardly a major

---

[1] New York World, July 22, 1877.
[2] Frederick Lewis Allen: *The Great Pierpont Morgan* (New York: Harper & Brothers; 1949), p. 224.
[3] Dulles: *Labor in America*, etc., op. cit., p. 234.

strike took place which was not pictured as a struggle between Americanism and Bolshevism.[1]

Free public education, free public highways, votes for women, child labor laws, reclamation of land, social security, comprehensive Federal health insurance [2]—practically every major reform of the last century—encountered the same hysterical opposition. Many of the political and social concepts accepted as pillars of the American way of life were denounced—at least by those who had a financial stake in abuses which the legislation was designed to cor-

---

[1] A classic example was the San Francisco general strike of 1934, which began with the longshoremen as a protest against a corrupt hiring system and spread to other unions after the police had shot down pickets. Two days before the walkout, the normally reliable San Francisco *Chronicle*, on July 14, 1934, published this story:

"REDS MARCH ON
S. F. TO PREACH
REVOLT IN STRIKE

"Attracted by the local strike situation and its potential usefulness in the pattern for a red revolution, known communists in large numbers yesterday began a march on San Francisco from northwest states."

The source of these amazing reports of an impending revolution was given as the Southern Pacific agent in the small town of Dunsmuir, California, near the Oregon line. All of the six San Francisco and Oakland newspapers printed similar stories. On July 28, 1934, these newspapers boasted of the success of the hoax in a full-page advertisement in the trade paper of the industry, *Editor & Publisher*. The page was headlined "Dailies Helped Break General Strike." To their credit, the editors of this conservative trade journal found nothing praiseworthy in the fabricated red scare. An editorial in the *same issue of Editor and Publisher* said: "To read some newspapers one would believe, were he unsophisticated, that 'Reds' were behind every strike, instigating every labor move, heroically defending every poor man's cause, from the Atlantic to the Pacific."

[2] The intransigent, costly campaign of the American Medical Association against Federal health insurance used the same technique. In February, 1951, Dr. Elmer L. Henderson, AMA president, writing in the February 24 issue of the AMA *Journal* characterized prominent supporters of Federal health insurance as having "pinkish pigmentation (and that's a mild way of saying it!)." The pigmentations thus diagnosed included presidents William Green of the AFL and Philip Murray of the CIO, Methodist Bishop G. Bromley Oxnam, Mrs. Franklin D. Roosevelt, and playwright Robert E. Sherwood.

rect—as the handiwork of Marx and Lenin. Housing reforms were no exception.

Sixty years ago, long before public housing was ever discussed, property owners and their allies inveighed against the threat of "socialism" when Trinity Church was convicted of violating the New York City Tenement Laws. For failing to provide running water on every floor of a tenement building, the Church, then one of the largest owners of tenement slums, was fined $200.

Appealing on the ground of unconstitutionality, the Church was upheld unanimously in 1892 by the Court of Common Pleas.

"There is no evidence, nor can the court judicially know, that the presence and distribution of water on the several floors will conduce to the health of the occupants. . . . There is no necessity for legislative compulsion on a landlord to distribute water through the stories of his building; since, if tenants require it, self-interest and the rivalry of competition are sufficient to secure it. . . . Now, if it be competent for the legislature to impose an expense on a landlord in order that tenants may be furnished with water in their rooms instead of in the yard or basement, at what point must this police power pause? . . . *A conclusion contrary to the present decision would involve the essential principle of that species of socialism under the regime of which the individual disappears and is absorbed by a collective being called the 'state,'—a principle utterly repugnant to the spirit of our political system, and necessarily fatal to our form of liberty.*" [1]

---

[1] Health Department of the City of New York v. Rector, etc., of Trinity Church in the City of New York. 17 N. Y. Supp. 510, at 515. Emphasis supplied.

In the belief that liberty need not be wholly divorced from sanitation in order to survive, the New York City Health Department appealed. Eventually, the Court of Appeals reversed the decision of the lower court and ruled that a law requiring a landlord to provide running water on every tenement floor was not unconstitutional.

3

For most slum landlords, laws compelling them to provide running water and sanitary toilet facilities were socialism enough. But when the government began to subsidize construction of low-rent public housing in 1937, real estate men succumbed to an epidemic of hysteria that has persisted to this day. "United States Housing Authority projects now under way are undiluted socialism," said the National Association of Real Estate Boards.[1]

From 1939 until 1949, the well-financed and ably led real estate lobby succeeded in blocking all Federal legislation to provide public housing for low-income families. During the war years, when labor and materials were required for armament and to provide housing for war workers, there might have been some excuse for withholding funds from civilian housing. But at the close of the war, when this country faced the greatest housing shortage in its history and returned veterans sought even slum dwellings in desperation, the real estate lobby proved its amazing effectiveness by bottling up public housing legislation

[1] *Confidential Weekly Letter,* December 26, 1939.

in Congressional Committees for four long years. This was a triumph of private greed over the public interest. It was achieved by a judicious invocation of the threat of "socialism" and/or "communism."

"I think the general adoption of a public housing building program means the end of this country, this life as we have known it," an official of the NAREB [1] said in a broadcast. "Trace back the history of every country that's gone Communistic or Socialistic, and it all started with public housing. It's Socialism pure and simple." Historians might point out that the Russian revolution was induced without any help from public housing, while Denmark, Sweden, Switzerland, and the Netherlands have built a lot of public housing and remained free enterprise, capitalist nations to this day.

But the real estate lobby and its faithful friends in Congress, undaunted by facts or history, continued the scare technique. Representative Ralph W. Gwinn (R., New York) took the floor of the House of Representatives on April 9, 1949, to ask, "Mr. Speaker, what ails America?" Answering his own question, he argued that socialism in housing was undermining our morals and, what seemed to him even worse, increasing the Democratic vote.

The Congressman continued: "As in Europe, the ruling party sees to it that the voting booths are placed conveniently in the basements of such government socialized housing. Alas, we have witnessed how American voters living in socialized housing projects cast a 90% vote, or more, in favor of the controlling party that builds the houses."

---

[1] Alexander Summer, chairman of the Washington Committee of NAREB, September 25, 1947.

Mr. Gwinn made three errors. One: elections in the United States are managed locally and Washington cannot control the location of voting booths. Two: public housing tenants do not vote 90% Democratic. Three: public housing is not built by any political party; it is built by local housing authorities which are non-partisan and almost always include in their membership Republicans, Democrats, and independents.

When the Housing Act of 1949 was eventually passed by Congress, Horace Russell, general counsel for the U. S. Savings and Loan League, called it "pure socialism." [1]

Although the real estate interests continued to scream about the threat of "socialism" and "communism" in public housing, the reason for their opposition was the fear that has always roused the foes of progress: fear of the effect on their pocketbooks. To some extent *these* fears may be justified.

In many southern cities, slum properties are expected to yield a return of 33⅓% on the investment each year. Many show an even higher profit. This bonanza is not, however, limited to the south. Real estate advertising in large northern and western cities shows that there is gold in the slums of all latitudes.

Here is a typical offering advertised in *The New York Times:* [2]

"3 BLDGS., RENT $10,200. PRICE $35,000.
CASH $10,000. PROFIT 32%."

---

[1] *The New York Times,* January 14, 1950.

[2] February 19, 1950. The buildings, on East Third Street, New York City, were, of course, "old-law" tenements, the kind of housing it has been illegal to build since 1900. In addition to six stores, there were in the building fifty-six cold-water flats renting for an average of $13.47 a month.

4

Just how "socialistic" is public housing? About as socialistic as public education, public sewer systems, public highways, flood control, the post office, fire departments, or any public enterprise.

Republican Senator Charles W. Tobey of New Hampshire demolished the charge in an exchange with a colleague who had opposed public housing on the familiar ground that it was "socialism."

"Did you vote for flood control down in your district?" Senator Tobey asked him.

"Yes."

"Did you vote for soil conservation and for free lime for farmers?"

"Yes."

"Did you vote for irrigation and drainage for farmers?"

"I did."

"Then will the senator kindly point out to me wherein those votes were not as socialistic as this legislation on housing, wherein the government advances money for public housing and slum clearance which, God knows, is sorely needed in municipalities throughout the country?" [1]

The truth is that a public housing program which substitutes healthful, livable, low-rent homes for miserable slums cuts the ground from under the Communists whose

---

[1] Told to the National Housing Conference on May 18, 1949 by Senator Tobey.

only strength comes from the failure of democracy to solve its people's problems. *Fortune* magazine expressed this political axiom as follows: "From a series of investigations . . . we have concluded that the . . . failure of capitalism to satisfy this elemental want [of a home] will do more to undermine free institutions than ten thousand Union Square orators."

5

The American constitutional system is probably the best government ever devised by man for orderly translation of people's needs into governmental deeds. Yet even our system has its weak spots. Understanding of these weaknesses can only increase respect for the fundamental soundness of the structure.

The belief is widely held that a bill which a majority of the members of Congress favor is promptly passed. The facts are to the contrary. A small minority can, and often does, temporarily thwart the people's will. This is how it works.

Every bill introduced into the Senate or House of Representatives is immediately referred to a standing committee. This committee may, after due consideration and public hearings, report the bill favorably or report it unfavorably and thus bring it before the whole body for debate and, eventually, a vote. Most bills are, however, accorded neither treatment. They are simply allowed by the committee to lapse and die.

When a bill has been introduced and referred to the appropriate committee, its fate rests with the members of that committee.

This system, or some substitute for it, is essential to prevent an enormous mass of bills from being forced upon the attention of the entire Congress. Only by limiting the amount of legislation to which members must give their attention can the legislative process be made to function.

Since the House of Representatives is the larger and more unwieldly body, the power of the House committees is even greater than in the Senate. It is therefore on the House committees that lobbyists concentrate their attention.

Let us assume that a bill is introduced to improve housing conditions. If it involves the appropriation of public funds, the bill is automatically referred to the Committee on Banking and Currency. A majority of that committee will decide its fate. If 14 of the 27 members of the committee vote against the bill, it is, for practical purposes, dead.[1]

Thus, to prevent the enactment of any piece of legislation, a Washington lobby need not influence a majority of the members of the House or the Senate, but only a majority of the House committee which handles the bill. Fourteen Congressmen can prevent any housing bill from becoming law. *From 1939 to 1949, under the tutelage of the real estate lobby, fourteen members of the Banking and Currency Committee prevented any public housing bill from coming before the House of Representatives.*

---

[1] There is a provision in legislative rules for bringing a bill out of committee by action of the House of Representatives as a whole. The procedure is rarely used and even more rarely effective.

Most Washington lobbies, whether they protect vested interests in waterpower, insurance, oil, silver, cotton—or slums—aim to kill legislation their employers oppose. The easiest way to do this is by blocking it in the congressional committee to which the bill is referred. If that fails, the lobbyists have another chance to put up a roadblock to progress. Even after a bill is favorably reported by the committee, it must still be favorably acted on by the Rules Committee, which alone has the right to bring a bill to the floor of the House.

The tremendous power lodged in the Rules Committee enables lobbies to kill many bills which a majority of both Houses of Congress wants. The Rules Committee has 12 members. Any bill can be killed by 7 of them.

Curtailment of the power of the Rules Committee is essential to restore majority rule, the basic principle of democracy, in the halls of Congress.

There is still another technique by which lobbies strangle social progress. It is used as a last resort when other tactics have failed.

The work of government cannot be carried on without sufficient funds. Appropriations for the technical and administrative expenses of every government agency are studied, analyzed—and eventually approved—by the Bureau of the Budget. The funds, however, are not available unless voted by Congress. Thus, if the Appropriations Committee—or rather, the sub-committee dealing with that particular agency—denies it adequate funds, its effectiveness is nullified.

A lobbyist will have not too much difficulty in persuading some member of the sub-committee to recommend a cut in an administrative budget. The member suggesting the cut may be moved by a sincere belief that the amount approved by the Bureau of the Budget is excessive. Or, the member may propose the cut as a sure way to steal a newspaper headline as a "champion of economy in government." Often, however, the cut is proposed—and adopted by the Appropriations Committee—directly on orders from a reactionary lobby. Having sought in vain to block enactment of the reform, the lobby thus succeeds in blocking its administration. A government agency deprived of adequate funds is helpless.

6

How does a lobby influence the individual legislator?

It is far from being a matter of obvious pressure or vulgar threats. Things are arranged much more adroitly. The lobbyist becomes personally acquainted with every member of the committee handling legislation affecting his employers. Real estate lobbyists make friends with members of the Banking and Currency Committee of the House of Representatives. That is their business. That is what they are paid for.

Over a cocktail, or at dinner, the lobbyist casually mentions that a certain bill is unfavorably regarded by the U. S. Savings and Loan League, the National Association of Home Builders, and the National Association of Real Estate Boards. If the legislator knows anything, he knows that this interlocking lobby mails a weekly newsletter to the local real estate board in virtually every community in the country.

Real estate board members are usually men of means and influence. They have a natural affiliation with local officers of insurance companies and banks; they are advertisers of consequence in the local press.

If Congressman X is a lawyer, he will hesitate to antagonize the financial and business interests to which he must look for clients. If he is in business, he will hesitate before opposing the local banker to whom he must look for loans. If he is a white collar worker, a journalist, or a teacher, similar considerations will influence his judgment. Congressman X will do a lot of thinking before he casts a vote which might make enemies of influential members of his home community.

To say this is not to reflect on the Congressman's integrity. Acting from the first of human laws, self-preservation, he may easily convince himself that his presence in Washington is too important to be jeopardized by a vote for a single piece of legislation, however sound it may be. Many good citizens who might criticize the Congressman would act no more selflessly in a similar situation. It is unfair and unrealistic to expect our public servants to maintain standards beyond those generally regarded as normal in private life. So Congressman X is apt to respond to the suggestions of the real estate lobby and oppose the bill.

If he hesitates, word is quickly passed through the real estate lobby's channels to his home town. He is then subjected to the treatment known as "turning on the heat." He will be invited back home to report to the people, usually by some large contributor to his election campaign.

The lobby will engineer a flood of letters and telegrams. He will be deluged by communications from his district urging him to vote against the "dangerous communistic" housing bill. So the Congressman will realize—if he has not before—that rich and powerful enemies are threatening his political life.

Where can he look for friends? A few sincere well-meaning citizens and a few civic organizations may rally to his support, doing the work on a volunteer basis, or assisted by a small underpaid staff. Matched against experienced, well-organized, well-financed real estate interests these are puny adversaries.

If Congressman X still refuses to desert the cause of better housing, other unsuspected obstacles may confront him. Not only will reactionaries and vested interests oppose him, but even many of those who stand to benefit most from the housing legislation. It is not at all unusual —and the author speaks from personal knowledge—for the people who live in the shacks and tenements of a blighted area about to be cleared for a low-rent housing project, to allow themselves to be organized by the real estate interests and slum landlords as a protest group *against* the program.[1]

Carefully planned propaganda may induce the potential

[1] When a county board in Miami, Florida announced plans in April, 1951 for rezoning a blighted area to make way for a new public housing project, Negro and white residents alike turned a public hearing into a stormy protest session, according to an account in the *Miami Daily News*, April 6, 1951. One resident objected to removing the blighted areas because they included "birthplaces of Negroes fighting in Korea." Another speaker assailed the administration in Washington, and, when told that Washington had nothing to do with the decision, asked if he could mention Russia and Communism. The president of the Negro Chamber of Commerce objected to the removal of the blighted area because, although the property had little value in dollars and cents, the homes were "covered with buckets of paint put on at night after a hard day's work."

beneficiaries to desert the congressman who has risked his political future for their sake. People are naturally conservative. Many are ill-informed, timid, and easily misled. It is not difficult to make them fear and resist change. When election day rolls around, Congressman X may find that his courageous stand on better housing for his constituents has cost him the election.

7

This description of the lobby and its methods with a recalcitrant congressman tells only half the story. The Washington lobbies—conspicuously the real estate lobby—operate in a much more positive way. They enlist the active co-operation of members of Congress.[1]

The right to send out mail without paying postage, the so-called free franking privilege, is one of the prerogatives of every senator and congressman. Originally intended to enable members of Congress to communicate with the

[1] Lobbies cover almost every field of legislation. For instance: "Speaker Sam Rayburn warned the President about the powerful lobbies fighting the price control bill. One of the most active of them, the National Cotton Council, fathered such a flood of amendments that it had to set up a shuttle system to get them introduced in the House. . . .

"Ray Blake, vice president of the Council, stationed himself near one of the less-public entrances of the House. From this vantage point he would hand a flock of amendments to Rep. W. R. Poage (D. Tex.). . . . Lobbyist Blake wore a bright blue necktie so that congressmen who didn't know him personally could identify him." Robert S. Allen in the *New York Post,* July 12, 1951.

people in matters of public interest, the postage-free frank
has become a tool of the lobbies. A lobbyist need only
have the sympathetic support of one or two congressmen
to be able to send out millions of pieces of mail for its own
ends—at the taxpayers' expense.

Since passage in 1946 of the law requiring registration
of lobbyists and the 1950 investigation of the House Select
Committee on Lobbying Activities, these abuses have
finally come under public scrutiny.

*One lobbyist admitted that his organization had distrib-
uted between 8 and 10 million propaganda pieces through
the mails between 1946 and 1950 under the postage-free
frank of congressional friends.*[1]

Another witness testifying in the probe of lobbying revealed his discovery of 4 million pieces of propaganda in
the corridor of the New Office Building of the House of
Representatives. The literature was assembled in the fold-
ing room in 800,000 envelopes for distribution in bulk to
mailing services employed by the same lobby.[2] Included
in the mailing were 450,000 pieces against rent control,
450,000 against public housing, 450,000 against Federal
Aid to Education. According to the witness, the entire
shipment was going out under the postage-free frank of
two congressmen.

One exhibit produced in the investigation showed that

---

[1] *Hearings Before the House Select Committee on Lobbying Activities,*
House of Representatives, 81st Congress, 2nd Session, Part 5, p. 98.
Dr. E. A. Rumley, executive secretary of the Committee for Constitu-
tional Government. This organization operates from expensive offices in
New York City. Its apparent purpose is to sow suspicion among the
people and to inculcate hatred of our government and its officials.

[2] *Hearings Before the House Select Committee,* etc., op. cit. Part 2,
pp. 223, 224.

a single congressman, with only 280,000 people in his district, had mailed out 900,000 postage-free franked letters containing 2,250,000 copies of speeches against public housing, rent control, etc.[1]

Among the legislators who allowed the most extended use of their postage-free franking privileges by the lobbies were Senator Harry F. Byrd (D., Virginia); Senator James E. Eastland (D., Miss.); Representatives Ralph W. Gwinn (R., New York), Wint Smith (R., Kansas) and Clare E. Hoffman (R., Michigan).

Until a few years ago, the price a legislator paid for defying a powerful lobby was usually his seat in Congress. Today, a courageous liberal who can dramatize the issues stands a chance of survival. Much of this change has come about from the appearance on the scene of organized labor as a potent political force.

Just as traditional lobbies—the power lobby, the real estate lobby, the oil lobby, and others—spend most of their time *blocking* liberal legislation, the labor lobby is occupied with promoting it. This is not to claim that legislation espoused by the great labor organizations is uniformly wise or desirable. But, by their very nature, the labor organizations are primarily concerned with the welfare of millions of people who are their members. Housing legislation, for instance, is a matter of special concern to labor because the cost of shelter represents the largest single expenditure made by union members.

While the drive which lead to the enactment of the United States Housing Act of 1937, establishing the first

---

[1] Ibid, p. 1164. For further information on the manifold activities of the lobbies, as well as the misuse of the franking privileges, see the entire proceedings of the *Hearings Before the House Select Committee on Lobbying Activities.*

permanent public housing program, was spearheaded by the American Federation of Labor, all branches of organized labor are now working effectively and harmoniously for improvement of housing.

Today, thanks to organized labor, a congressman who defies the special interest lobbies knows he can count on powerful, well-financed friends. The emergence of organized labor as a champion of legislators who oppose ruthless, hitherto unopposed, lobbies has decidedly altered the political picture.

8

All the hullabaloo about socialism still failed to prevent Congress from eventually enacting the Housing Act of 1949 which provided for a low-rent public housing program. But the real estate lobby did not give up the fight. Defenders of slum housing merely shifted the battlefield from Washington to the states and cities.

The National Association of Real Estate Boards has stated its position in language which cannot be misunderstood: "We are unalterably opposed to socialized housing and have strenuously opposed the $15 billion socialized housing program. It is vital that efforts be concentrated through local and state action by referenda and other means to carry on the fight." [1]

---

[1] In the NAREB newsletter, HEADLINES, of December 5, 1949. Emphasis supplied.

Local campaigns against public housing are run by remote control from the national headquarters of the interlocking real estate lobby. Week by week, syndicated scare propaganda, mats of canned editorials and cartoons are supplied free of charge to the newspapers wherever public housing is an issue. Identical advertising lay-outs appear in community after community; only the name of the town is changed.

Pamphlets, brochures, and cartoon books are supplied out of an ample central stockpile. The entire machinery of the real estate lobby has been geared to prevent the public housing law enacted by Congress from fulfilling its purpose.

Local opposition is stirred up by using the traditional scare technique of "socialism" and "communism." The line of attack varies little from the campaigns against public education a century ago. A few specimens of the kind of advertising which the lobby supplies free to newspapers throughout the country are reproduced here. The real estate lobby seems to have unlimited funds at its disposal for such purposes.

Other facets of the real estate board strategy were displayed in a typical campaign to defeat a referendum on public housing in Miami, Florida. "The opposition . . . put up the dirtiest fight imaginable," according to an account in the June, 1950, *Newsletter* of the National Housing Conference, Inc. "First of all they [opponents of public housing] were able to get a man who had started a one-horse credit reporting bureau to make credit reports for them—it is believed for the express purpose of making fictitious and false reports on the income of [public housing] tenants.

"Many of these reports were similar to the following. One man reported with a $9000 per year income, living in Liberty Square, had been dead for three years and never made over $35 per week. In another case, a man was reported as earning $75 per week and this man had been in

Private Enterprise is taking care of CITY NAME HOUSING NEEDS!

FINANCING PLANS

CAPITAL

BUILDING MATERIAL CATALOGS

SUPPLIER

LABOR

LOCAL BUILDERS, suppliers, financiers and labor working together have made new houses available since the war at an excellent rate and at attractive financing terms.

Since 0000, 000,000,000 building permits have been issued for the construction of new homes, the modernization of existing structures and for commercial building. Postwar building activity has been 00% higher than the pre-war period and every new house occupied has made additional housing available for others.

Can the people of ----- afford to lose the tax revenue from government-owned properties and at the same time furnish adequate police, fire and health protection, schools, streets, and other municipal services to these units? Can private homeowners be expected to pay their own costs of housing and also the expenses of the government housing tenants? During the past 000 years, real estate taxes on residential property have increased 00%!

Is it wise to tie ourselves up for a program of at least 40 years based on housing needs of today when private enterprise is rapidly overcoming our housing problems?

VOTE AGAINST GOVERNMENT SUBSIDIZED HOUSING!

SPONSORED BY

"Fill in your City Name here," says the United States Savings & Loan League, as it peddles free "canned" advertising layouts for use in the local press from coast to coast. It is all part of the interlocking real estate lobby's remote-

an insane asylum for more than two years. Another was the case of a Negro man reported working for $40 per week and his wife working as a clerk in one of our leading department stores at $35 per week. A check with the de-

THE TROJAN HORSE IS BACK!

GRAFT

POLITICS

SOCIALISM

FALSE PRETENSES

BRIBERY

THE GREEKS defeated the Trojans by sneaking a wooden horse containing armed soldiers into Troy. The soldiers descended from the horse, massacred the unsuspecting Trojans and set fire to their city. Victory was achieved by trickery.

Government housing represents a Trojan Horse of sinister consequences. Masquerading under neat phrases such as slum clearance, low cost, and houses for the needy, the program hides its socialistic implications. Karl Marx in the Communist Manifesto stated that abolition of private land ownership is the first step in the socialization of any country. The Socialists know that no American will vote for Socialism outright but through this housing scheme and other programs they entice Americans to accept their program bit by bit.

The announced policy of housing officials is to build government housing projects for the most part on vacant land sites with slums to remain! The Housing and Home Finance Agency estimates that our local community contribution for this program will be 50% of that of the Federal government. Is this free?

We must destroy this Trojan horse before it destroys us!

VOTE AGAINST GOVERNMENT SUBSIDIZED HOUSING!

SPONSORED BY

control campaign to undermine the Housing Act of 1949 at the community level and prevent the law from fulfilling its purpose.

partment store revealed that they did have a white woman of the same name working at that salary but living in an entirely different section of the city. Actually the man's wife was not working and had a two-week-old baby. There were many other cases just as ridiculous.

"The Local Housing Authority called on the County Commissioners to have their auditor make a complete check of its tenant-occupancy. After working three days, a team of three men reported that the Authority was run in accordance with law and administrative procedure. On the eve of the referendum, the chief spokesman for the opposition (author of the faked credit reports) made a radio statement to the effect that the Authority, and its executive director in particular, had been reported to the District Attorney and an investigation of the Authority demanded—all of which was pure bunk."

The real estate lobby's operations in this one city are described in detail because they are typical of the techniques employed to confuse the issues and mislead the voters in nearly every community which seeks to obtain Federal aid for slum clearance and low-rent housing.

9

It would be idle to deny that such tactics have not delayed progress. "Socialism" and "communism" are effective epithets which mislead the ignorant and frighten the timid. Housing legislation was blocked for years—at the cost of needless suffering and human misery. Yet there is a brighter side. Most reforms thus attacked have eventually been carried out and are now part of the accepted pattern of American life.

Moreover, there is growing realization among voters

that the citizen who would fulfill his duty as a free man in a free nation should learn the workings of his government. He must understand how the people's will may be nullified by the forces of reaction. He must be alert to the need for safeguarding the democratic process.

If the citizen is to be effective in promoting legislation for human betterment, he must know the obstacles and how to meet them.

Public housing for low-income citizens has at last surmounted bitter opposition and been accepted by Act of Congress. Today it is the law of the land. Extension of Federal aid to provide housing for middle-income families has been temporarily blocked by those who label it "socialism" and "communism." But victory in the long struggle to provide every American with a decent home is in sight. American families in need of an expanded housing program—two-thirds of a nation—can look to the future with confidence.

Appendix A

HOUSING RENT CHART

By

WILLIAM CHARNEY VLADECK, A.I.A.
Former Chief of Planning,
New York City Housing Authority

WHEN a residential low-cost rental housing project is in the planning stage, one question constantly haunts the planners: how much rent will we have to charge per room per month if the project is to pay its own way?

There are at least eight factors which combine to determine the eventual rental cost per room per month:

1. Density: number of persons—or families—to be housed on each acre.
2. Land cost.
3. The interest rate on the borrowed capital.
4. The period of amortization.
5. The cost of maintenance and operation in terms of dollars per room per year.
6. The cost of construction in terms of dollars per room.
7. Tax payments.
8. The annual loss for vacancy and collection costs, in terms of a given percentage of the annual rental revenue.

If, for example, a city housing authority were planning

a rental development and there were available cost estimates on all items, the rental per room per month could
certainly be figured out, but only after lengthy recourse
to higher mathematics. By the time this computation were
made, the variable costs might well have changed. It
would obviously be of great advantage to have a simple
means of determining, for instance, how much the theoretical rental would be raised if the density were lowered
by several families per acre. Heretofore it was necessary
for the entire calculation to be repeated.

The appended graph was developed to supply a simple
short-cut which avoids lengthy mathematics and still
supplies an accurate answer to the problem. Most of the
cost factors are involved in the charts. Once the total of
these items has been determined, it can be used as a lump
sum figure. The role of the remaining factors in determining cost can be worked out by relatively simple arithmetic.

The procedure for obtaining the rent per room per
month, based on these cost factors, can be outlined as
follows:

1. Draw a straight line through lines A, B, and C of the
chart to determine the land cost per room.

2. Draw a line through lines E, F, and G of the chart to
determine the annual debt service factor.

3. Connect the points where the above two lines inter-
sect lines C and E of the chart, and read on line D the
basic rent per room per month.

4. Make adjustments, if necessary for changes in:
   a. maintenance and operating cost
   b. changes in development cost (other than land
      cost)
   c. full tax payment

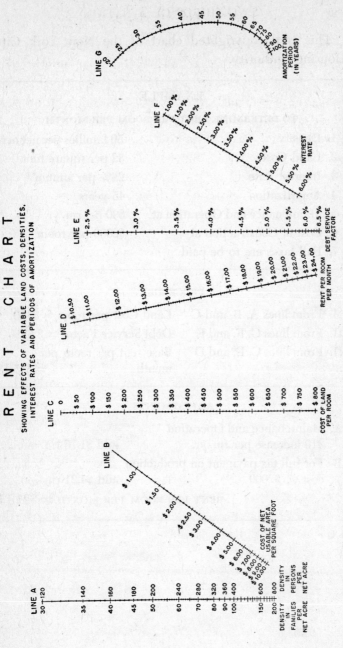

NEW YORK CITY HOUSING AUTHORITY
RENT CHART
SHOWING EFFECTS OF VARIABLE LAND COSTS, DENSITIES,
INTEREST RATES AND PERIODS OF AMORTIZATION

LINE A — DENSITY IN FAMILIES PER NET ACRE

LINE B — DENSITY IN PERSONS PER NET ACRE / COST OF NET USABLE AREA PER SQUARE FOOT

LINE C — COST OF LAND PER ROOM

LINE D — RENT PER ROOM PER MONTH

LINE E — DEBT SERVICE FACTOR

LINE F — INTEREST RATE

LINE G — AMORTIZATION PERIOD (IN YEARS)

Reproduced by permission of the New York City Housing Authority and William C. Vladeck, A.I.A.

This is a copyrighted chart of the New York City Housing Authority.

EXAMPLE

TO DETERMINE RENT PER ROOM PER MONTH

1. Density   50 families per net acre
2. Land Cost $2 per square foot
3. Interest Rate   2½% per annum
4. Amortization   45 years
5. Maintenance and Operation at $90 per rm/yr.
6. Cost of Construction at $2000 per room
7. Full taxes are to be paid

PROCEDURE

I. From lines A, B, and C   Land Cost per room = $440
II. From lines G, F, and E   Debt Service Factor = 3.69%
III. From lines C, E, and D   Base rent per room per
                              month   = $15.18

ADJUSTMENTS

A. Maintenance and Operation
   $10 increase per rm/yr.   add $1.76 rm/mo.
B. For full tax payment on production
   cost @ $2000   add $4.21 rm/mo.

RENT PER ROOM PER MONTH = $21.15

Appendix B

[These quotations are compiled from a magazine article by Sir Raymond Unwin entitled *Land Values in Relation to Planning and Housing in the United States*, dated January 20, 1940, published in *The Journal of Land & Public Utility*, February, 1941, and from Sir Raymond's own notes for his lectures delivered at Columbia University in 1939.]

LAND VALUE

"Land is valued for two main classes of use: first for the production of useful or enjoyable produce, whether food, game, raw materials or precious metals; second as affording sites for dwellings, industries, and commercial or social activities generally. The value in both classes consists in what folk are willing to pay for the privilege of using the land. . . .

"In the first class, a limit is set by the extent of produce which any land will yield over and above the costs of production, including the maintenance of the producers. This class of value attaches mainly to rural land . . .

"Values in the second class attach mainly to urban land and are usually far higher than those in the first class. These values depend on the extent of population and of the activities, on the importance of being near the center

of them, and the possible profit to be made by occupying the more favorably placed sites in preference to
others. . . .

"In both classes, the real values only exist if, and so long
as the land is used, and the buildings on it are occupied
for the respective purposes which create those values.
Where the land is not used, or where the buildings are not
occupied, no actual value is being created, and no real
land value exists. There will, of course, be a hope of future
value in the heart of the owner; there may even be an expectation of such value which seems plausible to his mind;
but until realized by actual occupation and use, both
values are speculative, not real. The hopes or expectations
of the owners may indeed be shared more or less by others,
and a market for the sale of land based upon them may
arise. This however, does not alter the fact that no real
value exists; that what is sold and bought in such market
is merely the chance to benefit by a hoped-for value, if it
is ever realized. . . .

"This aspect of values needs to be stressed, because the
very rapid development of population and urban centers
during the last century conferred an unreal appearance of
actuality on such speculative values."

DENSITY—KEY TO PLANNING

"Where increased density is secured by adding to the
number of storeys, that is, by piling more families above
one another on the same ground, there is a seeming avoid-

ance of part of the increased costs of development. This avoidance is, however, seeming rather than real, and largely consists in shifting the cost from those responsible for the development to the broad shoulders of the public. High density of occupancy throws greater demand on all streets and services to an extent not easily measured or allocated but very substantial.

"There is, however, one aspect of the matter which can be quantitatively stated. A certain space per 1,000 persons is regarded as necessary for recreation in urban areas. The smallest standard generally regarded as satisfactory calls for 7 acres of space per 1,000 persons, i.e., 33.88 square yards per person, or 127 yards per family of the size of 3.74 persons here taken. With 12 houses to the acre, 300 yards per family are available; so that the 7 acres per 1,000 for recreation ground could be taken and yet leave 173 yards available for private enjoyment by each family.

"In the higher densities, however, no such provision could be made, and additional land must be found from some source for recreation space. In the case of the density of 100 families to the acre proposed for certain housing schemes, to comply with the standard, 12,700 square yards or 2.62 acres must be provided for every acre used for building. If this land is to be reasonably accessible, it will have to be bought in the neighborhood, at prices based largely on the expectation that 100 families to the acre could be housed on it. For every acre thus built upon, therefore, there should be added to the cost the price of another 2.62 acres to be acquired for recreation space. Where high densities are permitted this cost usually falls on the public, through their parks committee.

"In this country there is more experience in urban conditions of high density than of low, especially for the low-income groups. In England, on the other hand, there is ample experience of both high and low densities for such dwellings. The whole municipal housing scheme [1] there affords a notable example. Of the 1,150,000 dwellings built by the local authorities since 1919, about 1,000,000 have been built at an average density of 12 to the acre. The larger land owners were able to appreciate the value of realizing increment on a larger area, and often accepted a lower price per acre in view of the restriction. . . .

"Supposing double the density had been adopted, a somewhat higher price would certainly have been asked in some cases. Assuming the same price, the owners would have lost half their increment; the tenants would have lost two-thirds of their gardens or recreation space . . .

"Congestion of families one above another does not materially affect the total of land values, but tends to concentrate that value on a smaller area. What the few owners gain in the center by concentration, the many lose on the outskirts. The effect of planning is mainly to change the *distribution* of value, and only to a much less degree to change the total. Good planning should tend to increase the total by adding to the efficiency of life and industry.

"If 40 storeys are adopted in place of 4, for example, approximately one-tenth only of the area of land will benefit by the realization of increment. The general adoption of higher buildings, coinciding with the diminishing rate of general expansion, must undoubtedly share responsibility for the prevalence of blighted areas round the business centers of many American towns.

----

[1] "Municipal housing scheme" is the English equivalent of "public housing program conducted by local authorities." N. S.

"From the above considerations and facts there would seem to be urgent reason for the citizens of New York and other American cities, as well as for the owners of land, to consider whether they would not all be far better off if they adopted a greatly reduced density of development accompanied by a reduced price per square foot of land, which, realised on a much larger area, would yield a greater total of value to owners, and would redeem blighted areas, not only at a greater speed, but in a manner which, because of the additional amenities and greater opportunities for recreation, would be much more likely to arrest the drift of population from the areas and secure their permanent occupation."

Index

A NOTE ON THE TYPE IN WHICH
THIS BOOK IS SET

The text of this book is set in Caledonia, a Linotype face designed by W. A. Dwiggins. This type belongs to the family of printing types called "modern face" by printers —a term used to mark the change in style of type-letters that occurred about 1800. Caledonia borders on the general design of Scotch Modern, but is more freely drawn than that letter.

The book was composed, printed, and bound by Kingsport Press, Inc., Kingsport, Tennessee.